KIRSTIN'S STORY:
no place to stand

KIRSTIN'S STORY:
no place to stand

JEAN JARDINE MILLER

JM
PUB-
LISH
-ING

National Library of Canada Cataloguing in Publication

Jardine Miller, Jean, 1945-

Kirstin's story : no place to stand / Jean Jardine Miller.

ISBN 0-9731376-3-0

1. Miller, Kirstin, 1972-1991. 2. Jardine Miller, Jean, 1945- —Family.

3. Anxiety in children. I. Title.

BF723.A5M44 2003   155.4'1246   C2003-907127-8

Cover and text design: Design and Copy Consultation Services.

Cover illustration: Kirstin Miller 1989

Poetry: *Songs of My Soul* by Kirstin Miller. ©Jean Jardine Miller 1992.

Jardine Miller
--publishing what is significant to today
Limehouse, ON L0P 1H0

PRINTED IN CANADA

*Dedicated to all bereaved parents of children
who could find no place to stand.*

PREFACE

I originally started to write this story a few months after my daughter's death. It was a therapeutic exercise – an attempt to make some sense of what had happened. I was able to see the earlier years fairly objectively and, while it was difficult, I could write about them. Time was needed before I would be able to get the later ones into perspective.

Often the pain seemed worse as the years went by. I wanted to finish the story but could only manage a bit at a time. For a long time, I just kept it on my computer without attempting to finish and edit it, or even correct the spelling. It was just an exercise that was supposed to help me, but really didn't.

Then, a visitor to the website I maintain for the assistance of people with anxiety disorders and their families, asked me for material that would help in explaining his daughter's school phobia to her teacher. He didn't know anything about me... he'd probably just stumbled onto the website after putting *anxiety* or *phobia* into a search engine. We were about to enter a new millennium, yet his child was experiencing the same lack of understanding that had virtually crippled my child's education in the nineteen eighties. Her father was searching the internet for help. Parents were still having to educate the very people who should have been the first to recognise the problem; the people who should have access to programs that could potentially prevent it from escalating... And I thought things had progressed.

Maybe I should finish telling my child's story. Perhaps it would help; make people aware of childhood anxiety disorders; let desperate parents know they are not alone...

But I'd never find anyone to publish it. I'd have to self-publish which meant limited distribution. It would be considered self-serving – no matter how hard it was to do. Anyway, it would be too difficult, emotionally, to edit... No, I couldn't do it.

Then I thought of a way, whereby writing the missing parts could be postponed, but which would force me to eventually write them and finish the story. I would serialise it in *Lifeline*, the quarterly anxiety disorder newsletter I published. Then I would publish it as an e-book and make it available from the website... perhaps even get it printed, eventually.

So, I finished writing the story.

Jean Jardine Miller
July, 2002

1

Dear Diary:

On Sunday the 21st, Robbie and I
got gerbils. Mine is named Chips.
Robbie named his Ketchup. On
Thursday, I went to the Kortright
Centre. I made a kite. On Friday, I
had to go and see "Robin Hood".

March 29th, 1982

Kirstin was nine years old when she wrote about the events of Spring Break in her Grade IV school journal. The journal is much like any other child's journal – a rather concise account of activities at Girl Guides and Sunday School, of ballet lessons, movies and television programs, having friends over and visiting their homes – all the ordinary things that are a large part of all our lives. It includes a running commentary on the development of her poster collection, experiences with teenage baby-sitters, what we had for supper and what happened when the car broke down – not an uncommon experience during the recession of the early nineteen-eighties!

Then, with the end of March 1982, everything changed.

The journal entry for the day after the Spring Break report is primarily concerned with a difference of opinion

Kirstin had with the baby-sitter who had looked after her and her brother, Robbie, the evening before while I was at night school. After that, there are three half-hearted entries for April. Six entries were made in May. These mostly end with the complaint that Kirstin still did not have her gerbil – a reference to the baby gerbil promised to her by the local veterinarian who I had prevailed upon, early in the month, to try – unsuccessfully, as it turned out – to save Chips II from joining Chips and Ketchup who had made their way to gerbil heaven within weeks of their arrival. The promised baby was not yet ready to leave its mother. There is one entry in June.

Social phobia had begun with a vengeance and was destined to dominate our lives until the even greater threat of agoraphobia loomed six years later. The lack of entries in the journal contrasts ominously with the action-packed records of previous weeks and months and, in itself, provides indication of the calamitous impact the onset of Kirstin's problem had on all our lives.

Kirstin, at this time, had her own front door key and was allowed to come home from school by herself on condition that she didn't invite other children into the house. Her brother, Robbie, was in morning kindergarten that year and was looked after, in the afternoons, by a friend, Lorna, whose house was almost directly opposite our own home. This was a convenient arrangement because Lorna was always available for Kirstin if she needed her. On the Friday evening of that week after Spring Break, a neighbour phoned me to tell me that she had twice seen Kirstin sitting on our patio when she should have been at school. The first time she had thought she must be staying home due to sickness or that I was taking her to the doctor or dentist. The second time, however, she called over to Kirstin, who appeared to be dressed for school. Kirstin quickly went into the house. It certainly looked as if she was not where she was supposed to be – hence, the telephone call. I thanked her, and called Kirstin up from the basement family room where she and Robbie were watching television. She could not explain her actions, but admitted that, instead of going to school, for the last two days, she had come back home as soon as she was sure I had left the house. Withdrawn silence was the only response to further questions.

During the weekend that followed, she appeared to be quite happy. On Saturday morning she went to her ballet class, as usual, while Robbie and I did the grocery shopping. In the afternoon, we took advantage of the early spring weather and went for a walk along the nearby river, looking for signs of Spring , which had been a tradition of ours for several years in early April. We went to Church on Sunday and the children went to a movie with their father in the afternoon – a fairly regular custom since their father and I had separated two and a half years before.

The next morning Kirstin refused to even make a pretence of going to school. She was just not going to go.

"Nobody likes me," she said, dry-eyed, but earnestly. "There's nobody to play with and Mr. Lemmon says I write garbage in my journal. So why should I go?"

Apart from the last accusation – the teacher's action of several weeks before which, while, to my mind, not entirely appropriate for a teacher of nine and ten-year-olds had been intended to express dissatisfaction with a couple of journal entries complaining of boredom in the classroom – there is no indication in the journal, or in school reports prior to that term, that Kirstin had any problem at school. True, her chronic asthma had the potential to set her apart, but there were other children in the neighbourhood who had asthma and she had always been encouraged to consider it a fact of life rather than something that made her different. The advent of school phobia, in fact, coincided with a period during which the asthma was well controlled.

Robbie's friend, Adam, had called for him while Kirstin was telling me why she could not go to school and the two small boys left in time to play in the school yard until the bell rang. Kirstin was determined to stay home. After repeated explanations, punctuated by silences on her part and assurances that she was mistaken on mine, I tried to tempt her with an offer to drive her to school since there was, by this time, not enough time to walk. She was not interested. I called my office to say that I'd be late and then phoned the school principal. I explained the situation, an explanation which, even to my own ears, sounded quite illogical. Kirstin was not a child who had problems with schoolwork. On the contrary she was a bright student with above average reading skills and highly-praised artistic talent. I asked if I could see him and Kirstin's class teacher as soon as possible to discuss the problem.

This meeting was the first of several during the next few weeks. Despite protests on the part of the school, I asked for a school attendance counsellor to be contacted. In fact, I was rather surprised that I had to ask – I suppose I had been conditioned to believe that this modern version of the truant officer spent the day tracking down truant children, as opposed to a child's mother having to beg for his help. Actually the attendance counsellor was a woman and she did not manage to reinforce my stance, in that children were required to go to school by law, as well as I had hoped. The best we could do between us was to persuade Kirstin to do her work in a corner of the special education teacher's room. This teacher had taught Kirstin's Grade II class before going into special education and was, perhaps associated with happier days in Kirstin's mind. Whatever the reason, Kirstin was quite agreeable to spending her days there in preference to her own classroom.

To say that Kirstin's sudden strange behaviour was a surprise would be an understatement. I felt as if I had been slapped in the face. We had been so happy and I'd been proud of the close and frank relationship my children had both with me and with each other so that the vehemence of Kirstin's resistance to attending school with no valid explanation scared me. I took her to our family doctor who cheerfully informed me that the lack of mental health services in the Region of Peel (one of the country's fastest growing areas) made it quite impossible to get any immediate help. Something told me that his diagnosis – "it was something she would grow out of" – was not correct and I asked him to recommend a private practice child psychologist. This I could ill afford but I had to find somebody who could find out what was wrong and, more importantly, how to deal with it. He referred me to a clinical psychologist operating from her home on a street not far from our own home which, of course, sounded very convenient. Optimistically, I called and made an appointment to talk over the problem with the psychologist, not knowing that this was only the beginning of a constant – and unsuccessful – search for someone, something, anything to help Kirstin to control her fear.

The child psychologist was a woman of about my own age with a young son. As such, I was hopeful that she would be able to relate to my anxiety when I explained the problem. She did not seem terribly interested in me... well, she was a *child* psychologist. She did, however, seem interested in telling me that I was living under stress and, thereby, causing family dysfunction and should see a psychologist myself. I felt rather indignant since I had, until recent weeks, been experiencing some of the most stress-free years of my adult life. Deciding this was probably a standard recommendation made when taking on a new patient, I told her I would think about counselling for myself and took down the address and telephone number of an associate she suggested although, as it was, her proposed schedule of psychotherapy for Kirstin looked as if it would bankrupt me.

I took Kirstin for her first assessment session a few days later. She made no protest upon the discovery that I was not to be a participant and, afterwards, appeared to have quite enjoyed doing Rorschach tests, apparently – being an imaginative child – having come up with rather unique interpretations for them.

"It was sort of like the Cloud Game," she told Robbie and I, "only black instead of white to make the shapes more scary – but they didn't scare me. We could use paint and do it ourselves."

I wondered about the effectiveness of Rorschach tests on subjects who'd had a lot of experience with *The Cloud Game* – a game we played which involved making stories out of the objects we found in the shapes of clouds. The other 'stuff' she'd been given to do, she told us, was mostly just puzzles like the ones in the British children's comics my parents had regularly sent her and Robbie before they emigrated from the UK to Australia a year or so before. Anyway, she had received the impression that she was supposed to have found them difficult because there was time left over which she had spent drawing as she was too scared to go and tell the doctor she was finished. No, the doctor had not talked to her about school she told me in response to my question – she had not, in fact, talked to her very much at all, but she had liked the drawing and had put it on the wall for other kids to see. I was glad the assessment portion of the program was covered by my group health insurance because it was expensive and I was beginning to feel more than a little sceptical about the outcome. Hopefully, on the other hand, something of value would be determined from Kirstin's answers to the test questions despite their structure being so familiar to her.

The psychologist finished her assessment during the next two appointments and embarked upon a psychotherapy program designed to combat the overwhelming fear, the existence of – but not the reason for – which was now confirmed by the assessment. She also had meetings with the school principal and the attendance counsellor but Kirstin continued to spend the school day in the special education teacher's room. She was able to finish her allotted Grade IV work far more quickly working alone and spent much of the day assisting younger students with remedial reading and math. She quite enjoyed this. The fear she experienced in the company of her peers did not seem to extend to younger children.

Despite my attempts to get her back into the classroom, including the investment in designer jeans and other clothes to impress her classmates, Kirstin finished the school year in the special education room. The staff at the school was extremely co-operative, helping us to the extent of the teacher scheduled to teach the Grade V class the following year, taking Kirstin out to lunch one day so that they could get to know one another.

The problems were not only associated with school, however. The little girl, who had once talked of auditioning for the National Ballet School, would no longer attend the Saturday morning lessons she had been so enthusiastic about for six years. The excitement of the weeks leading up to the end-of-term recital was sadly absent. I missed the annual chore of sewing yards of net onto a leotard!

The Girl Guide mother and daughter banquet was held at a local restaurant. Kirstin was a little reluctant to get ready, but after I had picked up the baby-sitter who would be looking after Robbie for the evening, she seemed to be all right and we set out. She was fine – until we parked the car. Then panic overwhelmed her. Not knowing how to deal with it, I forcibly assisted her in getting out of the car and walking to the restaurant thinking that, once I got her inside with her friends, she'd settle down and relax. Physically manhandling her into the restaurant was embarrassing and didn't help anyway. I soon gave up and we went back and sat in the car. By the time she finally relaxed we were both in tears.

"Why," I asked, "are you suddenly afraid of people you've known most of your life? You went to nursery school, to story hour at the library with some of these girls – you've known them since you were four years old. I don't understand."

She sat mutely staring out of the window. I think, for me, the toughest part of the incident was the fact that the panic attack (not that we knew what it was at the time) had occurred despite the fact that she was safely with me. Since she had always ran away from school to home, I had been under the impression that our home, which I assumed meant me, too, represented safety. Yet, here she was, safe with me yet overwhelmed with fear. When I eventually suggested that we, perhaps, try again, she immediately began to stiffen. I gave up and drove home.

The next week Kirstin was invited to a sleep-over party by Natalie, one of a small group of girls who refused to let Kirstin sever all connections with her classmates. They had, on several occasions, obtained permission to keep her company during lunchtime and recess in the special education classroom. She seemed quite touched to have been included in the party and happily rode off to the party on her bicycle in the company of another of the girls. At 11:30 pm the phone rang. It was Natalie's mother – Kirstin seemed to be terribly upset about something, was vomiting and wouldn't speak. It was almost like a fit or something – could I come quickly? I checked to make sure Robbie hadn't been awakened by the phone, got the car out and drove over to pick her up. The fact that I'd had to leave my son alone in the house, in the middle of the night, excused me from having to spend time trying to explain to Natalie's parents. I told them I'd come and fetch the bicycle the next day, and drove Kirstin home.

School finished the next week and I took the children for a week's vacation to a lodge on Lake Couchiching. I could ill-afford it, but we had to have the opportunity to relax after the stress of the preceding weeks. We swam a lot and I started to teach them both to play tennis – and golf, on the lodge's little five-hole golf course. About to turn six, Robbie was a bit small for these particular sports, but we had fun anyway.

The economy was beginning to recover after the 1981-82 recession but, unfortunately, it was a little too late for me. I had been paying 21¾% interest on my mortgage for almost a year and, although this would be substantially reduced when I renewed, debts had accumulated and the struggle to maintain ownership of the house was no longer viable. A few days after we returned home I called a real estate agent and put the house up for sale. Whether a change of address would give Kirstin the advantage of a new start or make things even worse remained to be seen. The risk was one we would have to take.

* * * * *

2

Falling

The sky is falling on us all.
The air breathes softly
Through the poison;
Take my soul.

And the waves are breaking,
making, creating
and they call.
The silence sings to me;
We have nowhere left to fall.

I had enrolled both Kirstin and Robbie in an arts-oriented day camp at a nearby community college for the first half of the summer. Kirstin, particularly, had been looking forward to it despite her problems with school. She loved art and drama and could think of nothing better than having the whole day revolve around what she loved doing – she was not expecting to have any difficulty. They had attended a two-week YMCA day camp the previous year and enjoyed it. But panic attacks (it was many years before Kirstin's episodes of alternating hysterical immobilization and sheer panic were actually diagnosed as such) are not discriminating. They spoil even the things the victim really wants to do!

It took most of the four weeks for Kirstin to become familiar enough with her surroundings, the counsellors and the other children, to be able to relax and enjoy the program a little. This involved all the reluctance to attend, running away and refusal to communicate with staff and peers that we had experienced with school which, at least, ruled out any possibility of the problem being the school itself. It was, however, more frightening for me because the camp was situated in an area with which Kirstin was not familiar, making running away a lot more dangerous than it had been in our own community. The first day the unfamiliar territory kept her from leaving the area in the community college grounds being used for the camp, but on the second morning I received a call from her counsellor as soon as I arrived at my office after dropping the children off – Kirstin had left the premises and could not be found. I drove back over to the college. It was only five minutes away – one of the reasons for selecting it in the first place. I tried, unsuccessfully, to spot her among people and traffic, then decided that, since she would be too scared to go into such a highly congested area, she was more likely hiding somewhere on the mostly deserted college grounds. I found a public phone – these were the days before we all had cell phones! – and called my office to find that she had phoned but had hung up when she was told I was not there. I returned to the office and waited for her to call again.

22

KIRSTIN'S STORY: no place to stand

"Mummy?" said the tiny, frightened voice when the call finally came. "I'm in a call box just down from where you go in. Please come and get me."

Every effort had been expended in saying that much. I told her to stay where she was and I 'd get there as fast as I possibly could and prayed that nobody would come along and frighten her away before I found the call box. Fortunately I found it quite easily and took her home. The next few days were very difficult, but we kept working at it and, eventually, she developed a bond with a young counsellor, who worked extremely hard to win her confidence, and she began to participate.

An additional problem was surfacing. Robbie had been diagnosed as a hyperkinetic as a toddler and we were used to his high energy level and the kind of escapades that bring problems for such children. By the time Kirstin had settled into day camp, Robbie was out of control – at three o'clock in the morning on the sleep-over night, I was asked to come and fetch him and not to bring him back. Kirstin, I discovered, had – after playing charades – gone happily to sleep. It had taken almost the entire four week camp period for her to win control over her fear.

The next morning, I let Robbie sleep while I arranged to have him spend the day at a friend's house. Then I called my office to say I'd be late and sat at the kitchen table drinking coffee while I tried to think the situation through rationally. I decided there was no point in discussing the problem with Kirstin's psychologist – I could not afford to pay for her to see Robbie, too.

Then I had an idea. When we first moved to the area which, at the time, was in an early stage of development, the church we joined shared services with another congregation and I remembered that the wife of the minister of that church was involved in child counselling. But, back when the subject had came up in conversation with a mutual acquaintance – ironically while we were discussing the behaviour problems of a neighbourhood child and feeling rather smug about our own well-behaved, well-balanced children! – there had been no need to know where she worked. I was pretty sure that it was OHIP-funded, however. I looked up the phone number and called her home. Her husband remembered me – he was a fellow Volkswagen Rabbit owner – and I explained my problem. Grace, he told me was away for a few days but, if I phoned the Child and Family Services Clinic at the local hospital, which was where she worked, and explained that Grace had directed me to make an appointment, I'd be able to get it faster than if I waited to speak to her when she came home. I did as he told me, heartily congratulating myself on discovering how to circumvent the system – this was the route for which the doctor had told me I'd have to wait at least six months!

The following week I took both children to the Child

and Family Services Clinic where they checked out the toys and books while I told Grace how Kirstin had developed what appeared to be a compulsive fear of people, how the doctor had said there was no help available and, at my own insistence, had referred me to a clinical psychologist who had assessed her and, had since then, been seeing her once a week for nearly three months. I admitted that there had been no improvement but, possibly, another few weeks would enable Kirstin to reach a greater comfort level and benefit from the sessions. Meantime, Robbie was exhibiting a behaviour problem that had ended in his being expelled from day camp and I needed someone to counsel him. She saw the children individually and then explained how the clinic operated on the premise that one person's problem impacted on each member of the family and, therefore, counselling must involve the whole family. This really seemed to make sense. Robbie was six years old – how could he be expected not to act out when his sister was getting so much attention for unacceptable behaviour? Indeed, why hadn't the psychologist considered it? If she was making the slow, but certain, progress with Kirstin that she claimed, she must know something of Robbie's behaviour problems. I felt like terminating the sessions immediately but knew that psychotherapy could not be handled that way. I decided to begin family therapy with Grace, but continue Kirstin's program with the psychologist. Grace agreed that three months, in terms of therapy, was not long enough to evaluate its success and, while she could not guarantee that Kirstin would benefit from the two forms of counselling, her program would not jeopardize the individual therapy.

Summer ended and school began again. Robbie, who was starting Grade I, was still young enough for me to have a plausible excuse to accompany the children on the first day of school but, of course, I was really there to provide encouragement for Kirstin. Robbie soon ran off with his friends to wait for their names to be called by the Grade I teachers and, mercifully, Kirstin's new teacher came over and, after asking Kirstin about what she'd done during the summer – not minding that Kirstin was too nervous to reply – kept her beside her while she called the names of the rest of her Grade V pupils. They all went into the school. I walked back to my car, fervently praying that everything was going to be all right.

For a little while everything was!

Sometimes mornings required a lot of effort, but Kirstin did go to school – and to her classroom – during those September weeks before we moved. However, she refused to register for ballet and attending Girl Guides was difficult and only really maintained because it was all she had left in common with her best friend of primary school years, Pamela, whose family had moved away from the immediate neighbourhood.

Now we were going to move, too. A series of mischances resulted in making a difficult situation more difficult. I had accepted an offer on the house with a completion date for the end of August but, due to the prospective purchaser not qualifying to assume the renewed mortgage, we understood the offer to have been withdrawn. I could not risk paying the first and last month's rent on the house I was proposing to lease and then find it necessary to make mortgage payments, too. I was in limbo for several weeks – the real estate agent continuing to bring new clients to view the property. Then, out of the blue, we were told that alternative financing had been acquired and the accepted offer stood. Fortunately, the real estate agent was able to get the completion date postponed, but I ended up in the unfortunate position of having to move less than a month after the school year began and being unable to find a house to rent in the immediate neighbourhood. The house I did find was not too distant but, unfortunately, far enough away to necessitate changing schools, although still close enough to maintain ties with Beavers, Girl Guides, the church we had attended since moving into the area six years before and, of course, the children's friends.

The weekend of our move was fun for the children. The last time we moved Robbie had been a newborn baby and, while Kirstin had participated, she had no clear memory of the move. Packing and unpacking, taking furniture apart and putting it together again was fun. Having new bedrooms in which to arrange possessions was fun. And negotiating the mud on the still unlandscaped lot was even greater fun. Going to school on Monday morning, however, was not fun.

I tried to explain the problems we had been experiencing to the principal at the new school but, so far as I could see, succeeded only in coming across as making excuses for potential bad behaviour on the part of my children. I made sure that both children knew where to get the school bus which would bring them home then, mercifully Kirstin went with the vice-principal, to the classroom to which she was assigned. I was asked to take Robbie to his classroom where I was able to meet his teacher and introduce myself.

I had arranged to be home by the time the school bus arrived, during the first week, and waited anxiously at the front door for the children that first day. Robbie excitedly told me about his day – always a long process because he insisted on acting everything out. Kirstin listened to him in miserable silence which even her brother's impersonations failed to break down. When he had changed and gone out to play with some boys he had met on the bus, she told me that she wasn't going tomorrow – they didn't even have a desk for her! I couldn't believe it. How could they be so insensitive after I had spent half the morning ensuring that they knew about the problem Kirstin had been having with attending school?

The next morning Robbie went to off, with his new friends, on the school bus. After much persuasion Kirstin agreed to get up on the understanding that I would see the principal and discuss the possibility of her changing classrooms. We arrived at the school and waited to see the principal. Once again I explained about Kirstin's school phobia and why the fact that there had been no desk available was just about the worst thing that could possibly have happened. He apologised for the desk situation but quite obviously perceived me as a misguided, over-protective parent and was not about to have me tell him how to run his school. I persisted in attempting to communicate the seriousness of the problem and, eventually, managed to make him understand that wild horses would be unable to drag Kirstin into yesterday's classroom. He agreed to have the desk, which had now been acquired, placed in the alternative Grade V classroom.

We all three went to the classroom where the desk had been placed and the principal had two boys move it to the new classroom where he introduced Kirstin to the teacher and class. Immediately a boy sprang up.

"Hey – she lives next door to me!" he cried. "She's my new neighbour."

Kirstin smiled and began to relax. Maybe everything was going to be all right...

Of course, it wasn't... For a few days she would get on the school bus with Robbie and the boys next door then she would be overcome with fear again. Sometimes I'd arrive at my office, after taking her to school, to the news that I was to return an urgent phone call from the school immediately. I'd dash home again to find her somewhere along the two mile route from the school and I'd take her back to school again. Usually I ended up letting her stay home because, at least, I could go to work knowing she was safe. Sometimes it was impossible to get her to school in the first place. A new attendance counsellor was assigned to us and he, the school principal, Kirstin's teacher and Grace, the psychotherapist, all tried to find a solution.

Kirstin's visits to the psychologist came to an abrupt end at this time. I went to pick her up one evening and found her, in her Girl Guide uniform – she had been intending to go to Guides after the session – on the doctor's couch curled up in a foetal position, refusing to move.

"This is all you've achieved in six months?" I asked the psychologist incredulously and was told that Kirstin had withdrawn that night when she'd been told not to draw cartoon dogs because she appeared to be doing so compulsively. I told her that we would no longer require her services and saved myself a much-needed seventy-five dollars a week. Kirstin did not go on to Guides that evening.

Working solely with Grace, who adored her drawings (many, which she kept for years, were returned to me, by her successor at the clinic, after her death) and did not attempt to apply strange theories to them. Kirstin began to show some improvement. She would quite often get through a full week of school, travelling there on the school bus without giving in to fear but, at other times it took most of the week to work up to staying there for a day. On these mornings, I would patiently wait for her to get ready in slow, slow motion, drive her to the school and take her to her classroom where the teacher would be waiting for her but, often she'd leave at lunch time and walk home. I eventually gave her a key of her own again and arranged for her to phone me when she reached home. The school attendance counsellor didn't approve but could provide no alternative and I needed the peace of mind of knowing she was safely at home.

* * * * *

3

I've been here before
with nothing to hold onto,
and it's hard to hold on
when there's nothing to hold onto.

from Beyond This Station.

Just after Christmas 1982 I had to have an operation to remove a benign tumour. The children stayed with the family of their longtime friends, Pamela and Barbara, whose mother, Marion, had regularly looked after Kirstin and Robbie for several years from the time I started working again, when my son was a year old, until the family moved some months before Kirstin's problems began. It was not possible for Marion to get the children to their school, so they had an extended Christmas vacation. However, during the weeks of convalescence, while I gradually increased my working hours, Kirstin made a supreme effort to control her panic and go to school on the school bus... and stay there.

During the rest of the school year incidents of panic and withdrawal became fewer and less frequent, as did our appointments with Grace. When she followed the fortunes of Lee Iacocca's Chrysler Corporation turnaround in her simulated investment portfolio, Kirstin became the class's 'wealthiest' student and won the current issue of MAD magazine as a prize. When time came to make plans for the summer, Kirstin asked to go to drama camp. Having been an enthusiastic drama student myself, both as a child and as an adolescent, I was delighted although, under the circumstances, it was the last thing I expected. I pointed out that she would have to go by herself since Robbie was not old enough for the program and she said she was aware of that and really wanted to go. I registered her and paid the fee, resigning myself to forfeiting the money if she panicked and was unable to go. But she went, worked hard – both at the program and at controlling her fear of the unfamiliar environment and people – and won the junior best actress award for the session. I still have the certificate, along with several others that she earned as a participant of various performing and visual arts programs during the few short years before fear permanently won the battle.

I bought camping equipment that summer. We had not camped for many years because of Kirstin's asthma. However, since this had been well-controlled for some time and because I was intending to take the children to visit our relatives in Australia at Christmas time, I decided to try it again as a means to economical vacation weekends. We had a wonderful summer. The children loved camping and we made excursions up north to cottage country, to

Kingston, Upper Canada Village at Morrisburg and Ottawa, as well as to staying in a Niagara Falls campground to do all the things that don't fit into a day trip, exploring Niagara-on-the-Lake and visiting the Brock Memorial and the Welland Canal. When September came, Kirstin had gained some self-esteem and was ready to face the new school year.

Perhaps if the school had not been so overcrowded, she would have been more successful, but this year was even more overwhelming than the last. Portable classrooms sprouted around the perimeter of the school yard and, to make matters worse, the Grade VI classrooms were in the senior part of the school surrounded by – for Kirstin – threatening grade seven and eight teenagers. The teacher tried to befriend and help her, but Kirstin's fear began to cause her to physically lose the ability to communicate and severely affected her concentration. For the first few weeks, she did most of her schoolwork at home in the evening, where she could relax enough to do it. Then, later – when panic prevented her from working in the classroom – she was allowed to work in a small storeroom instead. For a few weeks she attended a drama class run by a young man who had been a counsellor at the summer drama camp but, each week the fear of the other participants eroded her desire to act a little more until I could no longer persuade her to go at all. The same was true of Girl Guides.

I bought our dog, Buffy, at that time. Inevitably the necessity of my continually having to persuade, cajole and bribe her to go to school, as well as her own guilt over the constant stress her problem created, resulted in Kirstin perceiving these efforts to be conditions to my loving her. I hoped that the dog's strictly unconditional love for her would help her to feel more loveable herself. Again, I risked her asthma getting out of control, but felt it was a risk worth taking. And it was – she was very happy drawing, writing and talking about her dog and Buffy's affection elevated her self-image.

Most of the school-day, however, was still being spent in her own corner of the classroom and, during really tough days, in the little storeroom where the school principal had placed a desk for her in order to persuade her to, at least, stay on the premises.

Back during the first week of 1983, upon being told that the tumour, which had been removed along with my left ovary and Fallopian tube a few days before, was benign, I determined that we would go to Australia for Christmas that year. There's nothing like being confronted with your own mortality for the motivation to do the things you would otherwise postpone for years through lack of money!

My retired parents had emigrated, in 1981, from England to Campbelltown, New South Wales, where my sister and her family had lived for several years. We had not seen them since the summer of 1980, when we visited them in England and went to Scotland with them. Seeing each other only every two or three years, it was not possible for my parents and my children to know each other well, but mail and telephone contact had always been maintained. I suppose my renewed appreciation of life had also served to bring my parents advancing age to my attention. Whatever it was – I was anxious that the children know and remember them while they were still relatively healthy and active.

My sister, Lorna, had left England for Australia not long after I left British soil myself, for Canada, in 1965. She and her family, therefore, were only voices on the telephone and people in photographs for Kirstin and Robbie.

The proposed trip was, quite possibly, a factor in Kirstin's increased control of her condition during the first part of the year, in that she quite definitely achieved status among the children at school when she talked about saving money to visit relatives in Australia. For girls, particularly, peer approval during the pre-teen years has phenomenal impact upon self esteem and – in the years before *Neighbours* and *Home and Away* brought Australia into living-rooms around the world – this was a trip into the unknown, something that inspired envy! However, by the same token, the anticipated fear involved in meeting her unknown cousins, in all likelihood, contributed to the deterioration in that control during the months immediately prior to our departure.

When the long-awaited day of our flight to Sydney arrived, since I worked close to the airport, I took our luggage to the office with me and checked it on my way home, then picked the children up from school and took Buffy to the boarding kennel where she would be spending Christmas. The current gerbils had been left with Pamela and Barbara the previous evening. Leaving the pets, naturally, caused a little despondency in both of the children – the house felt strange in its pet-less state as we gathered together our cabin baggage and waited for the taxi to take us to the airport. Once they were aboard the plane for Honolulu – the first leg of our long journey – with Hawaiian music filtering through the cabin, visions of poor Buffy left at the boarding kennel soon gave place to the excitement of being en route to their first Australian Christmas.

My nephews, Trevor and Kevin, who were the same age as Kirstin, were as excited as my own children about meeting their cousins for the first time. Kirstin need not have worried – the four of them got along well together. They were soon adopting each other's accents and vocabulary, teaching each other how to play baseball and cricket and exchanging stickers – the big pre-teen hobby at the time. George Lucas's *Return of the Jedi* had just been released and the three pre-teens were not yet too old to have graduated from the childlike enjoyment of inventing their own space adventures and seven-year-old Robbie – ever the expert at imaginative story lines – was accepted as an equal in spite of his tender years! We did our Christmas shopping and had our picture taken with Santa, ordering an enlargement as a keepsake for my mother. It's a nice photograph. We all look so alive and happy – my mum's children and grandchildren.

Despite the challenge of socializing with her cousins' friends at parties, swimming events and even staying overnight with the twin sister of my older nephew's best friend, Kirstin had only one panic attack while we were there. This happened outside my parents' apartment when we were waiting for Lorna, her husband John, the boys and their friends to meet us on the way to a nearby park to play cricket. The game had been arranged the day before and the children had been looking forward to showing the Australian kids that they knew how to play cricket. But Kirstin was hiding by the time the others reached the apartment building and I was still trying to decide how to deal with the incident. I had explained about Kirstin's condition to Lorna, but none of the others had any idea that my pretty blonde, blue-eyed daughter had such a problem. Robbie ran over to join his new friends and Lorna came towards me.

"Where's Kirstin?" she asked.

I told her that Kirstin had gone into one of her

withdrawals – which is the way we described, and perceived, the problem at that time – and suggested she give me directions so that they could go ahead and we would come along later. After a consultation with John, she came back and asked if I would mind if she stayed – maybe she could help. I told her it was more a question of being patient and waiting, but she was quite welcome to see if there was anything she could do.

Kirstin had tucked herself into a corner where two walls of the neighbouring church joined. She was seated on the ground with her head hidden in her arms which were wrapped tightly around her knees. Lorna and I went to sit down on the grass beside her.

"The best thing to do," I told Lorna, "is to just carry on as if this is all quite normal and she'll eventually relax and come out of it. If you try directly to make her get up, you'll make things worse. Include her in the conversation, but don't directly refer to her sitting there like that."

After a few minutes, my father came along the path to go to the nearby store. The last thing I wanted was for my parents to get involved, so I got up and went over to him before he saw us. The whole concept of Kirstin being rigid with fear was incomprehensible to him – his generation was of the 'a good smack-bottom will teach you' school of dealing with unacceptable behaviour in children! He quite obviously thought I had been reading too many 'newfangled' parent guidance books when I tried to explain what we were doing but he, eventually, went on his way. Lorna decided that, since she still had the bag of refreshments, she had better get over to the park. After another half an hour the rain, which had been threatening all day, began to fall quite heavily. I told Kirstin that I was going to run for cover in the little covered mall where the stores were located. I looked over my shoulder as I reached the mall – Kirstin was running towards me, relaxed and looking almost happy as the heavy rain drenched her.

So the incident passed. That evening, after the children had gone to bed, my mother brought up the subject and I tried to explain the problem to her and my father, but I could not make them understand. It was as much a mystery to them as the fact that I did not allow my hyperkinetic son to have food colouring and chemicals, thereby ruling out the candies grandparents love to give to their grandchildren. Due to the fact that they did not often see us, they tended to think I imagined – or, maybe, even caused my children's behaviour problems. It was depressing. I wished there was somebody who understood. The trip did, however, provide for Kirstin, Robbie and me the luxury of having an extended family for two weeks. Until recent years I had never really appreciated the value of being part of a family. Yes, I had missed having a family, but had not fully understood the importance of the support and reinforcement it could provide during life's tough times – at least, not until trying to cope with Kirstin's problem left me feeling so very much alone. The children were both a little homesick by the time we boarded the plane to go home again, but excited because we were about to do something which very few people get to do – see the New Year in twice. Due to crossing the International Date Line on January 1st, we welcomed in 1984 first in Campbelltown then, again, as our plane took off from Honolulu.

Home again, Kirstin's fear of school resurfaced – intensely. The public school environment had become just too overwhelming. I came to the realization that the system just did not have the resources to deal with Kirstin's condition. I began looking for an alternative school where, hopefully, a low teacher-pupil ratio would be less threatening for her. I had heard of one quite nearby which a short time before had used our church facilities while waiting for a new building to be completed. I asked Grace about it and, while its primary focus was upon teaching children with learning disabilities, we decided it might just be the right place for Kirstin to develop the self-esteem that was needed to combat her fear.

I met with the school's director and explained the problem to her. She told me how the school had developed out of the tutoring and remedial program she had administered some years before for children with learning disabilities. I was shown around the school and introduced to the junior level remedial teacher, to whose class Kirstin would be assigned. Five children were working independently in the small, cheerful room. I was impressed by the atmosphere – surely she would be happy here...

I arranged for Kirstin to attend the school as a visitor for the next few days. Amazingly, she almost immediately bonded with the teacher and was not afraid of the children. Now it was just a matter of finding the money to pay the fees! If I could enlist the help of her father, I could manage it. He had experienced the impact of one or two of her panic attacks but, like most people, had no conception of the full extent of the problem. Fortunately, Grace had decided that it was about time he participated in some of our family therapy sessions. The first time he did so, she presented the case for Kirstin attending the school and outlined the need for him to assist with the financing. She did a far better job than I could have done myself and Kirstin was formally enrolled in the new school the next day.

During the first six months of 1984, she filled in the many gaps created by her erratic school attendance in the previous three grades and finished her Grade VI year working at Grade VIII level. There were, of course, difficult days – days when getting to school took an enormous effort, days when running away was easier... but the admiration she received as a result of the sketches she wrote, directed and acted in for the school's Spring Festival created new confidence and her school journal for those months paints a picture of an observant, imaginative... and happy eleven-year-old.

* * * * *

4

84.06.23

Dear Mom,

*I am not getting bored out here. In fact,
with the ants, crabs, slugs, snails and
snotty-nosed kids sticking their fingers
in the ice cream, I'm fed up. I hope you
liked the necklace. That's abalone or
however you spell it. I went to Alert Bay
today with Auntie Nola and Uncle
Doug. We saw the biggest totem pole in
the world...*

By the time the 1983-83 school year ended, Kirstin's self-confidence was high enough to enable her to fly alone from Toronto to Vancouver, where she was met by her paternal grandparents and taken to the small island community of Sointula for an extended visit with her aunt and cousins. Even taking into consideration the fact that Kirstin was well-travelled due to our family members being dispersed in various countries around the world, this was a major undertaking for a child of her age and we were all very proud of her achievement. The idea had come about because Stephanie, her new friend at school, was flying alone to the east coast to visit relatives for the summer. Kirstin decided she would go west and help her aunt with her young family in BC. I tried to dissuade her from committing herself to the two month visit she was suggesting but Stephanie was leaving as soon as school finished so nothing would do but for Kirstin to do so, too. I knew she would be helpful entertaining her six and seven-year-old cousins because she was very good at creating imaginative games to play and she was also at the age when small babies (her infant cousin was six months old) become quite fascinating. Two months, to my own mind, however, was long enough for the novelty of being 'the big cousin come to stay' to wear off. But she became stubborn and would not be persuaded. It was almost as if she had selected the scheme as a test for herself which she was determined to pass. I realised that it was like drama camp last year – a case of come hell or high water, she was *going* to make it work.

And she did.

I missed her, and many times – talking to her on the phone or reading her letters – wanted to go and fetch her home but I knew that, however homesick she became, she was determined to stay. Perhaps it was a case of needing to be successful at things that really were hard to do because that would somehow make up for all the things which were easy for everybody else but created panic for her.

Robbie and I flew out to British Columbia to pick her up at her grandparents' Nanaimo apartment, where she spent a week after being brought down from Sointula by her aunt. Robbie slept while I drove the rented car from the airport to the ferry terminal, but was wide awake and hungry by the time we boarded the ferry. The apartment building was just a short drive from the ferry and Kirstin was waiting for us in the entrance hall. She and I cried happy tears as Robbie looked on disdainfully – male eight-year-olds are not noted for emotional reunions.

The first evening Robbie stayed with his grandparents while I took Kirstin out to dinner. It was so good to be together again. She had enjoyed the summer, despite the stress of having to control her fear of new places and people, and was proud of the achievement. She confided that she would be glad to get home again and, ruefully, told me that I had been right – two months was too long!

We stayed in Nanaimo for two days. My father-in-law was anxious to show us the scenic spots around his newly adopted home – they had moved there only two years before – and both grandparents wanted to spend some time with Robbie. Kirstin and I explored the museum and other cultural tourist attractions of Nanaimo. A nearby go-cart track was a big attraction for both children. Kirstin and her grandfather had, apparently, already had lots of practice during the previous week. Robbie, to his chagrin, was too young to ride by himself, but soon discovered that riding with Grandpa was just as much fun.

We left on the early morning ferry to begin our drive

across British Columbia to Banff where I had made reservations for us to stay at a mountain resort for several days before driving on to Calgary and flying home. The first leg of the journey took us up the Thompson Valley to Cache Creek where we booked into a motel complete with swimming pool for the children to work off their excess energy. We were up early again the next morning, driving to Kamloops before stopping for breakfast, then crossing the Okanagan and visiting Glacier National Park on our way to Banff.

It was another idyllic holiday – one of happy days exploring the hiking trails around the resort, visiting and hiking around Lake Louise and buying souvenirs in the Banff stores. We took the cable cars up into the mountains, the children laughing at my vertigo until I recovered once we were at the top – at least, until it was time to go down again!

The last morning of our holiday we drove to Calgary. I always manage to meet up with a traffic officer when I drive a rented car and this time was no exception. This one came out of nowhere just as we began to leave the mountains behind us. It's always mortifying to get stopped for speeding in front of your children!

"Never mind, Mom," Rob said as the officer handed me the ticket. "You don't have to pay when you're from out-of-town!" I quickly wound up the window.

We continued on to Calgary and visited the zoo where,

like many children before and after them, Kirstin and Robbie discovered the fascinating world of dinosaurs. Then we flew home. The only pictures we have from Kamloops, through the Rockies, to Calgary were those taken by Kirstin – I didn't discover that the film in my camera had snagged somehow until I realised, at Calgary Zoo, that I had taken more pictures than I could possibly have had film for!

Kirstin's determination to meet the challenge of her fear of unfamiliar people and situations did not extend to the long term. Yes, she could travel, by herself, to the west coast and visit relatives she had not seen for a long time. She could excel in a drama workshop or a Spring Festival. She could win admiration and respect for her artistic abilities. But she could not surmount the difficulty of facing the unknown when its end was not in sight.

This is a retrospective view. Kirstin's problem did not have a name until we had been battling it for almost six years. In 1984, it still came under that all-inclusive umbrella definition for children's behavioural difficulties – 'emotional disturbance'. It is not a term I ever used myself – for me it connoted, and still does, the anti-social behaviour of the abused and neglected children from a children's home, who attended the village school of my childhood in England, during the lean years after World War II. It intimates a tangible reason for the child's problem, one that was consciously created. It is a very over-used label employed, among other things, to provide a cause for school problems that does not suggest any fault on the part of either the school or the heatlh system.

If I had been able to see the short term success versus long term failure syndrome earlier, perhaps I could have developed a strategy that would have assisted my child. Instead I was as overwhelmed as she was and, however many books I read on child psychology – mostly out-of-date volumes from the shelves of the local libraries – there was nothing to guide me. And, even if I had come across the terms "social phobia", "panic disorder", "agoraphobia", such possibilities would have been discounted because I would also have read that these disorders were not supposed to happen to children.

Despite settling into the little private school and making friends prior to the summer and following that up with the hard earned achievements of the summer, returning to school, in the Fall, was still very difficult for Kirstin. Enrolled in a regular Grade VII and VIII class with twelve-to-one student/teacher ratio and a concerned and caring home-room teacher, the future should have been promising and, for the first few weeks of the term, she seemed to have little difficulty. The new computers, with which the school's director had equipped the school this year, were a great incentive, especially since children who arrived early were allowed to work with them until time came for classes to begin. Kirstin was fascinated by computers, and I could not yet afford to buy one for ourselves, so she was eager to get to school in time to use a computer. She maintained her friendship with Stephanie, although they were now in different classes, and they visited each other's homes at weekends. And she was working well – mostly at high school level, since she had finished most of the core Grade VII and VIII material the previous term – and enjoying the challenge of the work. However, at the junior high school level, subjects are no longer all taught by the same teacher and there were new and – from Kirstin's perspective – threatening class-mates. The overwhelming fear and panic began again.

Conditions deteriorated quickly. Robbie and the boys next door had become regular patrons of the local public swimming pool during Kirstin's absence. The weather was still very warm the first few times Kirstin went with them and they all wore their bathing suits to and from the pool but the days grew cooler towards the end of September, and it became necessary to change at the pool. Going into the ladies' change-room by herself was too difficult for Kirstin and she stopped going.

Concurrently, she developed a dislike for her history teacher – to the point of leaving the school and starting out for home instead of going to his classroom. School attendance, once again, became progressively more difficult.

We limped through October. Often, I'd take Robbie and the child of a neighbour with whom I car-pooled to school, then come home again to persuade Kirstin to get up and go to school. After her twelfth birthday in November, her school friends' admiration of a tiny hand-held portable television, purchased with birthday money and the proceeds of a matured savings bond, provided a stimulus for going to school for a little while. The novelty, of course, soon wore off and by the end of the month I was, once again, desperately seeking professional help for her.

It happened so quickly. It was hard to believe that this was the same child who – just a few months ago – had courageously and confidently spent two months far from home. Most disastrous was the fact that I no longer had the option (assuming I could find the money) of having Kirstin moved into a low ratio remedial class, where she could have worked independently, because the home-room teacher for the remedial junior high school class was the history teacher for whom she had developed the unwarranted dislike.

At the local hospital's Child and Family Services Department, Grace felt that the problem had escalated to a point where she was really no longer equipped to deal with it. Therefore, I asked the Director at Toronto's Hospital for Sick Children's Chest Clinic, where Kirstin had been an outpatient for most of her life due to her chronic asthma, to refer her for psychiatric assessment there. I obtained a referral and set up an outpatient clinic appointment which Kirstin and I attended. A case-worker interviewed me, while a psychiatrist talked to Kirstin. It took some persuading on my part – even with Grace's reinforcement – to make them understand that there was nowhere nearer to home for us to go. They finally agreed to set up a schedule of appointments for her that would mean making the journey to the hospital once a week.

Getting Kirstin to keep the appointments was even more difficult. It was Christmas time which meant that the first session was put off until after the holidays. Then, once regular appointments were established, there was no bonding with the psychiatrist assigned to Kirstin as there had been with Grace and, because there was little flexibility in appointment times, Kirstin's delaying tactics usually resulted in my having to re-schedule appointments. To add to our difficulties, she had begun to display the scary, irrational behaviour of cutting the hands and arms that mental health professionals refer to as 'slashing'. I was told that this was a desire to hurt oneself, born out of low self-esteem, and did not, in itself, indicate suicidal thinking. But it was scary – dreadfully scary.

Meanwhile, I was in the middle of buying a house again. I had first noticed the *For Sale* sign on the pretty little bungalow in Streetsville in early October. I watched as the price was lowered and the house became empty, then I went to the listing agent. My supposition was correct – the owners were on bridge financing and accepted my offer of less than they had really wanted. We were about to have a house of our own again – with a garden big enough to play baseball in without any risk to the windows, full of trees and bushes where forts could be built and a fenced area where Buffy would be safe without having to be tied up to prevent her from getting on the road.

The day before we were due to move we had a family counselling appointment with the new psychiatrist – these, Kirstin usually managed to negotiate more successfully because Robbie and I were present. I had taken the day off and arranged for Robbie to bring schoolwork home for the two days – Kirstin's school attendance, at this point, being almost non-existent – as I felt the move would be handled most effectively if we did it together.

I had already had possession of the new house which had needed a lot of cleaning before we could move in and, since our appointment was not until after lunch, I left the children to do some final packing with the promise of a restaurant lunch on the way to the hospital, and I took some things over to the new house – something we had been doing for several days in order to keep moving costs down. When I returned both children were missing. While I had had a lot of difficulty getting Kirstin to the previous appointment – it had been re-scheduled twice – she had seemed to accept the inevitability of today's appointment, even joking about getting Robbie the whole day off school, too! I was surprised and disappointed and tried to convince myself that they would be back in time to get to the hospital.

After I had scoured the neighbourhood both by car and on foot with Buffy, I stopped kidding myself. I no longer expected to find them before the appointment time had come and gone. I had some lunch, called the hospital to explain what had happened and re-scheduled the appointment, then decided to do some more moving, expecting to find the children returned when I got back. They weren't home, however, when I came back and I began to worry. One part of me rationalized that they had probably walked farther than they had intended and now had a long walk home ahead of them, but the other part was running scared. The usual mothers' worst imaginings began to fill my mind and I called the police.

Explaining the situation to the officer who came to take the report was difficult. I knew that the children had run away because Kirstin was afraid of attending the psychiatrist's appointment. But, in the officer's book, children ran away to have fun and were usually to be found at a friend's house – albeit that it was a school day and other children were at school – or hanging out at a shopping mall. It was impossible to make him understand that the children were far more likely to be in one of the many woodlots in the area, or down by the river, than at the shopping mall. He took photographs with him and went about looking for them *his* way. This was frustrating as I knew that he was not likely to find them and I had to stay in the house, myself, in case either the children or the police telephoned me. The rest of the afternoon and early evening passed slowly. I knew they were most likely making their way home, but was afraid that they had become lost either together or had quarrelled and become lost separately.

Eventually the door bell rang. It was a woman with Robbie. She had found him walking, by himself, on a deserted road and felt it hardly likely that this was what an eight-year-old was supposed to be doing on a dark winter evening. He was cold and wet and, as I ran a hot bath for him, he told me that they had walked all the way to the new house but couldn't get in. Then, they'd got hungry and cold and had had a fight about which was the fastest way home and split up. I made him some soup and leaving him with instructions to explain what had happened if the police called, drove the five miles to the house we would be moving into the next day. I checked both inside and outside the house but Kirstin wasn't there. A man came up the driveway as I went back to my car.

"Are you the new owner here?" he asked.

"Yes," I said.

"We had to call the police earlier this evening," he told me. "There were a couple of kids trying to break in..."

KIRSTIN'S STORY: no place to stand

In tears myself by this time, I attempted to explain what had happened. Another neighbour-to-be had joined us by this time and invited me back to her house to use her telephone. I phoned home to make sure Robbie was all right and he told me that his rescuer had returned and brought Kirstin with her and he had put the rest of the soup on to heat and was running a bath for her to get warm. I was so relieved and grateful for the kindness of the unknown Good Samaritan who had left as anonymously as she had arrived by the time I reached home again. As it happened, Robbie and I came across her a few weeks later in a local restaurant and I was, at last, able to thank her for her help. By that time, Kirstin was in hospital...

* * * * *

5

feel
How I long to feel the rain again
see
See the sun rise over the land again,
hear
Hear the calling of the distant shore
And walk toward the shining light once
more.

from The Shining Light.

During the first few days after we moved Kirstin was motivated to go to school – moving was a big event and there was so much news to share with her friend Stephanie! She organized her belongings in her new bedroom and arranged her poster collection in the basement room which we made into a studio for her. And she attended the rescheduled appointment at the hospital with Robbie and me.

For a short while I dared to hope that things were going to get better again, but she refused to attend the next hospital appointment and persuading her to go to school in the mornings began to take longer and longer until she, once again, stopped going altogether. Persuaded by the psychiatrist, who was handling her mostly unattended out-patient appointments at the hospital, I agreed to her being admitted for residential assessment.

Between the ages of two and four, Kirstin had been hospitalized on several occasions during asthma attacks, severe bronchitis and pneumonia to which she was prone. There had been times when I almost lived at Toronto's Hospital for Sick Children. However, these relatively short periods of hospitalization did not really prepare us for the four months that Kirstin spent on the Child and Family Services Ward in 1985.

On the day scheduled for her admittance to the hospital, I took the school principal up on her offer to pick up Robbie, who was happy to go to school early and have first choice of the computers. We took the little hand-held television set which could be plugged into the car's cigarette lighter – it helped to persuade her to get into the car, although I did not think there was much likelihood of her being allowed to have it in the hospital. On the way, I chattered inconsequentially about previous visits to the hospital – from ambulance journeys when she was younger to parking difficulties during outpatient appointments – while Kirstin mostly fiddled with the television's antenna.

Upon our arrival, the primary child-care worker assigned to Kirstin showed us around, took down a condensed version of her history and arranged for her asthma medication. Then it was time for me to leave.

When your child is physically sick and must be left in hospital, you feel bad. When your child is perfectly healthy and must be left in hospital, you feel awful – there's a sense of betrayal, a guilt trip, the feeling that you've failed your child. The other children were in the school room, but it would soon be lunch time and there would be group activities during the afternoon. Kirstin was not expected to participate yet, however, and was encouraged to familiarize herself with her surroundings instead. I left her drawing in her room. She refused to say goodbye and just leaned further over her sketch pad when I tried to kiss her.

"I love you, Kirstin. This hurts me, too, but I want you to get better," I said and, fighting back tears, made my way out of the hospital and back to my car. I cried during most of the drive to my office.

Kirstin was reluctant to co-operate at all during the first week, refusing to eat, wash or talk – except to ask me to take her home when I phoned or visited her. During the first weekend – which Robbie was spending with his father – I was able to spend Saturday evening at the hospital. When I arrived I found her playing Scrabble. Most of the children were at home for the weekend and the child-care worker on duty had been able to work with Kirstin on a one-on-one basis throughout most of the day. Kirstin had eaten both lunch and dinner and, starved for conversation, had become quite voluble as the day progressed. We played Scrabble and later Kirstin, at last, agreed to take a bath. Relaxed in the bathroom, she talked non-stop about her fellow patients, the nurses, the teachers and the child-care workers. For the first time, I felt almost comfortable about leaving when it was time for me to go.

We were all being subjected to far more intensive scrutiny than we had been previously. I resented the text book psychology, the invasion of privacy, the innuendo and the guilt trips but I hung in there because, somewhere in the midst of it all, perhaps some means of helping my child would be found. Kirstin, herself, after the first week or so, adapted quite well to the hospital environment. She soon had a roommate – who turned out to share the same birthday with her. They became firm friends and were allowed to decorate their room with pictures of animals and pop stars which they cut from magazines. She was popular with both teachers and children in the school-room because of her creative abilities and talent for teaching the younger children to read, a job she was given when her own work was finished. And she developed good relationships with the front-line child-care workers. Unfortunately the same could not be said for her relationships with psychiatrists and psychologists. This was to become an ongoing problem, in fact, since they, in turn, are generally not terribly well-disposed towards working with involuntary patients. At this point, however,

I was aware of neither of these facts and, perhaps, rather naively expected the psychiatrist to put more effort into winning my daughter's confidence instead of continually investigating *my* childhood, *my* marriage, *my* separation, *my* sex life, *my* career. In fact, I still have difficulty understanding this type of approach – which is favoured by many people in the profession – of attempting, and often succeeding, in totally demoralising the parents who voluntarily expose themselves to humiliating scrutiny in the attempt to find solutions to their children's problems.

After several weeks, Kirstin had her first 'pass' and I took her to dinner at the *Organ Grinder*, where we generally celebrated birthdays and other special occasions. She was relaxed and quite happily chatted about the other children and the child-care workers at the hospital and I told her about the plans for the Spring Festival at school and how, since she couldn't be in it this year, she had been asked to design the program instead. The next weekend, I was able to take her out again for a short time. This time Robbie came, too, and we went to the light show at the McLaughlin Planetarium. After that she began coming home for weekends.

This involved my having to pick her up on Friday afternoons, which sometimes presented difficulty for me and resulted in my having to take Kirstin back to the office and leaving Robbie home alone after school for longer than I really liked to do. I would return her to the hospital on Sunday evening when we would have to report the events of the weekend to the case-worker. It was a routine we had to learn to live with and it was, although we did not know it then, a forerunner to periods of residential treatment yet to come.

The hospitalization lasted until school ended and, upon Kirstin's discharge, we were referred to a psychiatrist, at a clinic closer to our home, for continuing psychotherapy and supervision of her medication. She had been placed on imipramine during her hospital stay and was expected to require the help it provided in keeping her mood elevated for some time to come.

Liaison between the hospital and our area board of education resulted in Kirstin being offered a place in a special education 'contact' class for children with behavioural exceptionalities for the next school year. Kirstin, herself, felt confident that she was well enough to be able to go to the local junior high where she would have the opportunity to renew acquaintance with some of the girls, such as her old friend Pamela, with whom she had gone to school in the years before her problem began. I agreed to postpone making a final decision until closer to the beginning of the school year.

She was glad to be home again permanently and, after a weeks' vacation which we spent at a friend's cottage, she began working in clay with a local sculptor who was running classes for children for the summer. Later that summer, both the children attended the drama camp where Kirstin had enjoyed such success two years before. This time, at nearly thirteen, it was harder to escape from herself than it had been when she was younger – even for children who do not have to cope with anxiety disorders, the teen years are not easy on self confidence and self esteem. However, she attended each day and coped with being primarily identified as the older sister of the ringleader of a group of small boys who were a continual bane to the camp leaders. Robbie, needless to say, had a great time. During the Civic Holiday weekend, a woman playing a guitar at a corn roast at the campground where we were staying, inspired her to begin guitar lessons.

During the last week in August, I made the decision about school and arranged for us to visit the school where the 'contact' program was run. We were able to meet the principal and the 'contact' class teacher. Mercifully, Kirstin immediately liked this lady (to whom I shall always be grateful for making what turned out to be Kirstin's last regular school year happy) and agreed that she would be far more comfortable here than at our local school. Because the program was designed primarily for children whose difficulties caused them to be disruptive in regular classrooms and such children tend to be boys, the teacher was happy to have a girl in the class and this, as it turned out, was the key to Kirstin having a successful school year.

Both the teacher and the teacher's aide were extremely caring people and the boys in the class became very protective of Kirstin. The regular teachers, whose classes she attended when she did not need the reinforcement of the 'contact' class, were also very supportive, especially the core grade eight teacher who continually praised her efforts. A group of girls, who took it upon themselves to help her, persuaded her to join them in the computer club, a bible class and even, for a short time, to play a trumpet in the school orchestra.

With above average marks in the core subjects, she was encouraged to apply for enrolment at an arts-oriented high school for the following year, where double credits were available in visual and performing arts. We put together a portfolio of her art for her interview, including a series of photographs which I took at the various stages of the development of the plaster head she sculpted using Robbie as her model during their Saturday morning sculpture lessons. The interview was one snowy Saturday afternoon in February and we waited several weeks to hear of the result. She was accepted despite – and, in fact, was the first student to be accepted with what the school system continued to define as 'having a behavioural exceptionality'.

With the help of medication, psychotherapy sessions each week, two caring teachers and a teacher's aide Kirstin finished elementary school with high enough grades in the core academic subjects to support her placement in the specialized high school arts program. Sometimes the going was tough. There were many mornings when she refused to get up in time to take the taxi which picked up children attending special programs. On these occasions, I'd sometimes manage to persuade her to let me drive her to the school and take her to the Contact Class. At other times I had to give up and let her stay home. The year was also not without its traumas. A boy died at the school during an asthma attack which was especially impactive for Kirstin, an asthmatic herself. Another boy – a member of the Contact Class – who shared her enthusiasm for *Dungeons and Dragons*, improved and was transferred back to his home school. And, at home, the difficulties of dealing with Kirstin's disorder began to impact on Robbie, for whom the progress from cute, mischievous little boy to more mature, responsible behaviour was proving difficult. However, we all made it through the 1985-86 school year and, at the end of June, proudly attended Kirstin's graduation. I took pictures of her in the pretty white dress for which we had so much fun shopping. Kirstin even went to the graduation dance with her classmates and enjoyed herself. Then her grade eight teacher – who lived near us and drove her home – took the entire class for a pizza supper. My own participation, of course, was limited to attending the graduation ceremony and taking photographs but, somehow, that evening still seems magical when I look back on it. Perhaps it was...

The school principal recommended Kirstin for an enriched arts program, provided by the board of education, which took place during the first half of the summer. Many of the children attending were also bound for the same high school arts program as Kirstin and we hoped that, perhaps, she would make some friends. This, unfortunately was not to be but she did graduate with certificates of excellence both in visual arts and drama. She was happy and proud of her achievements, none of which – despite her tremendous ability – came easily because of her fear of the unfamiliar surroundings. As usual, there were days when getting her there was difficult but we kept working at it. I remember being called one morning by the extremely alarmed program director who had never experienced seeing someone in the process of having a panic attack and it was hard for me to determine who needed calming most. Despite this unfortunate experience, however, the course ended with Kirstin participating in the final performances and the open house for friends and family. We added the certificates to the others on the wall of her basement studio and prepared for our holiday on Manitoulin Island.

We all enjoyed the holiday – including the dog, Buffy, who loved exploring new places as long as we were there with her. We had spent a couple of days in Little Current five years before on our way home from a trip to Moosenee but had not seen more than the east end of the island. This time, from our Elizabeth Bay base, we were able to explore the whole island and the surrounding La Cloche area – including a day at Science North in Sudbury. We were befriended by a couple, staying in one of the neighbouring cabins, who took the children out fishing in their boat and shared campfires with us in the evenings. One day, as we were driving back to our cabin from a day spent at the west end of the island, Kirstin and I saw a doe with twin fawns cross the road in front of us. Robbie was asleep with Buffy in the back of the car and they were gone before we could get him to wake up. Memories like this one of seeing the twin fawns are among the hardest for bereaved people because unique events must be talked about and, when they are no longer *shared* memories, they become especially poignant.

The museums on Manitoulin Island are great places for children to learn about the hardships of isolation and the Lake Huron shipwrecks of the last century. Perhaps, however, it was the spiritual Indian heritage that most impressed my children that summer. The atmosphere of such desolate rocky places as, for example, Misery Point, probably enters every visitor's soul. After Kirstin's death, somebody who only knew her through reading her poetry used the expression *an old soul in a young body* to describe her. Such an idea seems to explain why spiritual impressions permeate the whole being of some people more so than others. I think that, for Kirstin, the spirituality she found at Misery Point blended with such lasting impressions as a family bible used to exorcise a ghost which she had been shown, during a trip to Scotland some years before, to create a spirituality which gradually removed her from every day reality.

Home again, after the long drive from Elizabeth Bay, a more practical reality was overgrown lawns and weed filled borders and the local cat lady who appeared, as we unloaded the car, mistakenly accusing Robbie of throwing stones at one of her menagerie. It was an amusing homecoming despite the insult to Robbie, and created a light-hearted atmosphere in which to tackle the work on the house and garden that is always the aftermath of a holiday. It was still summer – time for Kirstin to be happy, but high school was around the corner bringing a new era of worsening anxiety and panic.

* * * * *

6

Lonely Days

Here I stand
lost and forgotten
Oh, oh lonely days.
A prisoner of the ground I've trodden,
I wove the web that now I'm caught in.

The School for the Arts program, for which Kirstin had been accepted, was provided at a high school some distance from where we lived. This meant that Kirstin, like most of the arts students at the school, was picked up by a school bus. Had it been otherwise, perhaps she would have had a better chance of settling into the new school. However, the twofold fear of teens on the bus and at the school proved to be completely overwhelming. Perhaps the outcome would have been more successful had her psychiatrist not stopped her antidepressant medication two weeks before – to this day, something I cannot understand. Yes, she was doing well, but starting high school is traumatic for any child – let alone one with a history of school phobia. I questioned his decision, but who was I to do so? Just her mother.

We tried very hard to make it work but, after the first

few days, she gave up trying to conquer the fear of the bus and, on the mornings when she managed to overcome fear enough to get up, I drove her to school. She managed the bus in the afternoons – simply, I imagine, because it was taking her to the safety of home.

Naturally, attendance became progressively more infrequent. Several mornings, I drove to the school only to turn around and drive home again – Kirstin was too paralysed with fear to even get out of the car. The situation was beyond the comprehension of the counselling staff at the school and my telephone calls to the board of education elicited only the fact that there were no relevant special education facilities within the system at the high school level. During the sixth week, Kirstin attempted suicide.

The evening before we had attended a psychiatrist's appointment and I had told him how I felt that his terminating the antidepressant medication had been premature and that Kirstin's loss of control was derived directly from that decision. I suggested she be put back on the medication – this from someone who is routinely anti-medication! He disagreed. In the face of his patient having regressed in six weeks to the condition that had prompted hospitalization little more than a year and a half before, I still find it hard to understand his attitude. It seems, however, to be the attitude of many members of the profession – all the time you object to a program, they insist it's the only way to go, while as soon as you come around to their way of thinking, they change their minds. It was this scenario which eventually proved fatal for my child – although not at the hands of this particular psychiatrist.

No, I had not been happy about Kirstin being given imipramine originally, but I recognized that it served its purpose in providing the assistance she needed in controlling both her anxiety and the depression it inevitably brought about. He, however, no longer appeared to do so. In Kirstin's presence, he counselled me to continue to stand firm in insisting she go to school. I knew he was wrong – there had to be another way. I remember the flight of fancy I had as I drove home that evening – that, had we lived in another century, none of this would be happening. That night Kirstin overdosed on aminophylline, the bronchial dilator which she took regularly, along with other drugs, to control her asthma.

The next morning I called her to get up. This was my normal procedure whether or not it resulted in her going the school. I always felt that if I began the morning on the assumption that our lives were normal, there was a greater chance that they would be. Sometimes it even worked!. Kirstin was always very wheezy when she woke up and required inhalation therapy. This morning, however, she was also choking and gasping that she was sick. I grabbed a bowl and took it into her room. Choking and vomiting, she told me what she'd done. I helped her to get her clothes on and I told Robbie that I'd have to get her to the hospital right away, assuring him that she'd be all right, but I needed his co-operation in getting himself off to school. Of course, in true small boy fashion, he was only too eager to get to school with the morbid news of his sister's attempted suicide. I left him finishing his breakfast and drove Kirstin through the rush hour traffic to the Emergency Department at the Hospital for Sick Children.

Although I had managed to remain calm in front of the children, what was filling my mind with horror was the fact that theophylline has been the murder weapon in a mystery movie I had recently seen on television. However, once we reached the hospital, Kirstin was given carbon to drink, put on an IV and was soon stabilized. Weak with relief, I was ushered away to be interrogated by social workers.

I swear that hospital emergency staff work under the assumption that a child's attempted suicide is strictly due to bad parenting. Coping with this attitude is very difficult when you are scared to death that your child may have caused irreparable physical damage to herself – and we're talking about an asthmatic child with weak, pneumonia-scarred lungs – not to mention the mental trauma. I explained what had happened, told them that she had been a patient of the hospital since the age of two and gave them her file number so that they could read the whole story, but they persisted in perceiving me to be some kind of abusive parent. In fact, they almost convinced me that I was.

Kirstin remained under medical supervision for the weekend, and became extremely popular with both children and nurses by drawing portraits of Sting, who was at the height of his popularity at the time, for them. Once medically fit, she was transferred to the Child and Family Services ward where she remained for several weeks.

This second stay in the residential Child and Family Services program was not as effective as the first one had been. I questioned the decision that she be admitted there rather than to its adolescent counterpart – after all, she was almost fourteen and a high school student now – and was told that it was felt she'd benefit more from the younger children's program. Since the school-room had run out of material for her, a year and a half before this was rather difficult to understand. They did not seem to realise that getting behind in her high school credits would be disastrous for Kirstin insofar as getting her back into a regular school was concerned – her fear of other teens was bad enough without getting unnecessarily behind her own age group. She was, once again, given the job of helping the younger children to read while the teachers discussed soap operas. Yes, this was wonderful for her self-esteem, but was scarcely helpful in learning to interact with children of her own age. My general perception of this hospital stay was that nobody really knew what to do. One recently graduated social worker suggested I give up my job and register for welfare so that I could attend school with Kirstin! While I was not, at that time, as familiar with anxiety disorders as I am now and Kirstin was still being treated primarily for clinical depression, it hardly took psychological expertise to know that such a step would even further alienate her from her peers.

Her friendship with a twelve-year-old boy who, like her, aspired to a fantasy world where reality was never contemplated, resulted in the two of them running away and getting lost in the hospitals' labyrinth of underground corridors. She was discharged. Hospitalization was not benefiting her I was told and, other than to recommence therapy sessions with her psychiatrist, there was nothing else they could suggest. I was not terribly surprised by this attitude – treatment programs all seemed to be designed around the patient conforming to the treatment rather than the treatment conforming to the patient. For instance, this residential program operated only five days a week. If not deemed fit to go home, patients in the children's program were shifted to the adolescent ward on weekends. So, whether she were to go home or stay in the hospital, for Kirstin each week had to be started afresh. By the end of the week, she was reasonably comfortable with the staff and patients. By Sunday evening, she was begging me not to take her back there.

Whether she summoned up the courage to voluntarily walk into the hospital or whether I literally had to drag her in, Sunday evenings were something of a nightmare for all of us. At the risk of sounding as if I did not want my daughter home, I had suggested that this one step forward and two steps back procedure was not very helpful. The only reaction was the one I received on any observation I made, whether on the impact of asthma medication, that of body chemistry, hypoglycemia or anything else on Kirstin's condition – my perceptions were of very little importance.

I was not about to take her back to the psychiatrist who, as far as I was concerned, had nearly killed her. Previously, I had been afraid not to have a professional administer her treatment but, now, that she had attempted suicide while under a psychiatrist's care, it no longer seemed so important. Perhaps a holiday from health professionals, altogether, was in order.

Kirstin was discharged from the hospital just before Christmas. In the New Year I started looking at private schools again. The first one I contacted suggested Kirstin attend for a few days on a trial basis. After meeting the headmaster and being shown around the school, she agreed to do so. Things seemed to go quite well the first day; the second morning she was unable to find the courage to get up. The headmaster took her absence personally. It was so hard to make people understand.

A few days later I discovered a small Christian high school where students worked at their own pace. I arranged to see the pastor. The non-competitive atmosphere appeared to be ideal for Kirstin and would solve the whole problem of having lost the entire autumn term. I was a little concerned about the fundamentalist principles of the school, but there were other children enrolled whose families did not belong to the Pentecostal denomination that administered the school and Robbie was currently attending a Baptist school whose staff respected the faith of the families of its non-Baptist students, so I convinced myself it would not present a problem. At a second interview, Kirstin came with me and met the pastor as well as some of the students and was offered a place for the following school year. Testing would be set up for both Kirstin and myself in June. In the meantime, I would have to administer her education myself.

This involved fending off the school board which, despite having no solution to offer us, persisted in having an attendance counsellor continually threaten me with court action for 'preventing' Kirstin from attending school. I, eventually, managed to communicate the position to the Superintendent of Schools and never heard from them again. I would set Kirstin work to do each day – drawn from a combination of what I knew the grade nine syllabus covered, *Coles' Notes* and what I remembered learning myself at age fourteen – and I'd mark it in the evening. She was well-read, eager to learn and the only difficulties we had were in some aspects of mathematics, which was never a strong subject for me – though I must admit sines and tangents now seemed to make much more sense than they had done twenty five years or so before.

At Easter we went to Nassau for a few days, where the children swam and snorkelled and played tennis. I just swam and played tennis, not being too fond of being fully submerged. We explored Nassau, bought souvenirs and generally put our troubles out of mind. Kirstin was relaxed, unafraid and happy – if there were only some way for life to always be this way... but we both knew that avoidance behaviour would never solve the problem.

Home from Nassau, we continued the respite and Kirstin remained in control of her disorder. In June, she spent two days at the new school completing the entrance tests. She seemed to get along well with the other prospective pupils and was assessed as being better educated than most children who transferred there from a public school. I attended the seminar for parents and had my religious knowledge tested – I got the impression that they had not expected somebody in the advertising industry to do very well, despite my having told them that I had taught Sunday School for many years. It was quite amusing when my Bible knowledge turned out to be better than any of the other parents!

The enthusiasm for tennis, which had begun in Nassau, remained with the children for the entire summer and extended to attending a tennis camp. In August, we took a camping trip to Quebec City. This included a visit to Saint Anne de Beaupré where we toured the Basilica and the Shrine Museum. Kirstin and I were both fascinated by the documented miracle cures. I wondered whether the pilgrims were all Catholic, whether Protestants could pray on the Scala Santa... I've always had a very confused perception of Catholicism being somehow superior to Protestantism. I prayed very hard at the miraculous statue instead, and hoped God wouldn't think I was being presumptuous. Kirstin had been happy during the months since she had been discharged from hospital. However, she had been in no other company but that of mine, Robbie, her father and her guitar teacher. Even at the tennis camp she and Robbie had played together. Her social circle could not be confined to her family forever. I suggested she earn the money for her guitar lessons by baby-sitting, bringing to her attention that her guitar teacher, himself, was a good place to start since he and his wife had three small children. After much agonising, she plucked up the courage to ask him and became the children's first choice baby-sitter. She began to really rebuild her confidence. Then September came around again.

The year started off well at the new school. The teacher was more a facilitator than a traditional teacher and the students worked by themselves, setting goals on a daily basis and learning by doing rather than being taught.

Kirstin learned well this way. Many of the children had to pass our house on the way to the bus stop to go home and Kirstin, walking with them, actually invited one or two of them into the house on several occasions. She became friendly with the pastor's daughters and was invited to their home. She found a new baby-sitting client when one of her classmates recommended her for a job she could not do herself. She was beginning to enjoy a normal teenage lifestyle.

But it didn't last. Perhaps it was stage-fright at the thought of playing her guitar in the Thanksgiving concert. Or maybe it was the visit to the ophthalmologist and being diagnosed as myopic. Whatever the cause, the uncontrollable fear returned and Kirstin, once again, became afraid to go to school. Both staff members and children from the school came to visit her. They all tried so hard to make her understand how much they liked her and valued her company, but she was not able to find the courage to return to school.

* * * * *

7

We cannot live without the Trees;
They contribute to the air we breathe.
We must ensure that they survive
So that all Creatures on the Earth
Can breathe, in harmony, together.
This is Peace. This is the Breath of Life.

from The Trees.

After the experience of the year before, another admission to the Hospital for Sick Children appeared unlikely to be beneficial and, in reacting to Kirstin's suicide attempt, I had burned my bridges with the last psychiatrist who had treated her. I tried going to our family doctor again and, this time he gave me a referral to a psychiatrist at our local hospital. Unfortunately, however, this doctor rarely visited his office and never returned my calls. I learned later that he was the Chief of Psychiatric Staff.

Some time previously a friend, whose own daughter had become a suicide victim after many years of trying to control the depression caused by bulimia, had given me the name of a psychiatrist who he felt had been of great assistance to her. *He* was in his office the first time I called.

He did not take adolescent patients, however, but suggested I call the Director of Adolescent Services at Sunnybrook Hospital. I turned his suggestion into a referral for administration purposes and obtained an appointment, then – thankfully – managed to persuade Kirstin to keep the appointment with me.

The doctor was doubtful about admitting someone from so far away as Mississauga for his observation program but, after I had told him the story of the past five and a half years, he set up appointments for Kirstin and me with the program's psychologist – the first step to an evaluation. Kirstin, mercifully, liked the psychologist – an Australian who, on finding we had relatives in his native land, was able to establish common ground with Kirstin and, eventually, persuaded her that a short stay in hospital would allow her condition to be properly evaluated.

A panic attack preventing her from being admitted on our first attempt. This failure was hard to take. I had the psychologist called down to the parking lot to help me. He made a few attempts to persuade Kirstin to come into the hospital with him but she remained rigidly in a foetal position refusing to speak to either of us. Finally he decided that perhaps the timing was wrong and we should wait and try again another time. I arranged to telephone him later in the day and drove home fighting tears.

"Why?" I asked. "You *wanted* to go. You *want* to get better. Why did you do that?"

"I don't know," she said, recovered now that the danger has passed. "It was like he said – it was the wrong time."

I called the psychologist and he set up a new admission plan involving our coming prepared for Kirstin to stay but leaving it up to her to decide, after he had showed her over the entire ward and introduced her to the other patients. She finally began the six week residential evaluation in late November.

By early January it emerged that clinical depression, which had always been the diagnosis, was not the problem in itself, but a symptom of social phobia. Long term – two, possibly three years – residential treatment, aimed at controlling the problem before it degenerated into full-blown agoraphobia, was the recommendation.

"Why have we never been told this before?" I wanted to know, feeling as if I'd been kicked in the stomach. "She's been treated for depression all this time – prescribed medication that... that was useless?"

The psychiatrist told me not to worry about the medication. Imipramine was considered to be effective for phobic conditions. Anxiety disorders were not well documented and it was not surprising that Kirstin had been misdiagnosed. In fact, it was generally the case with this condition. I learned later that he was actually way ahead of his time – social phobia was not officially recognised by the World Health Organisation until 1992, the year after Kirstin's death.

It was hard to accept that there was no easy answer –
no magic solution. I tried telling myself that it would be
as if she were at a boarding school. Once she had been
evaluated, she would have weekend passes. It wouldn't
be so bad. After all she was fifteen and two generations
before economics dictated that the majority of fifteen-
year-old girls leave school and go to work away from
home in apprenticeships or domestic service. She'd be
with other teens who had problems relating to their peers
and the rest of the world – maybe she'd even make
friends. I kept talking myself into believing it would work
– that the continuous behavioural and cognitive therapy
possible in the residential treatment environment would
result in Kirstin learning to control her fear.

At first Kirstin allowed herself to be lulled into a false
security due to having to wait for a place to become
available. There was every chance of it taking forever – or,
at least, until she was too old to be eligible! She went back
to being happy for a few weeks – staying at home and not
having to face the fear of school. Even after the application
for a place in the adolescent residential treatment program
at the Hincks Treatment Centre was processed and we
were interviewed, approved, had completed the myriad
of forms required and arranged the date of admittance,
she continued to block out the reality of the situation. She
did not believe she needed to go – she was perfectly
happy as she was. Trying to sound sincere and loving

while feeling that I was being perceived as smug and patronizing, I explained time and again that it was my duty as a mother – and as a human being – to do my best to ensure that she had every opportunity to become self-sufficient and I could not do that by letting her hide from reality. But how do you talk about sending your child to live away from home because you can't fix the problem the way you used to fix the scraped knees and hurt feelings of childhood – and retain credibility as a loving mother? She had to learn to control her fear – and I had to endure the fact that she hated me for making her do so.

She responded to my attempts at conditioning by blocking out the impending treatment program and, consequently, panicked when we were notified that a place would be available for her in two weeks. The two weeks were hard. Shopping for new clothes helped – the list of required clothing and equipment was surprisingly long due to the combination of school and recreation requirements. Then we had to ascertain that such 'necessities' as guitar and radio were allowed. They were, but group activities took precedence and there would little time to enjoy them.

The day arrived, all too soon, and I drove Kirstin to the city. I was able to help her to arrange her possessions on her side of the small room she would be sharing with an, as yet, unknown roommate – a girl of her own age who was at a stage of treatment where she was attending her local high school and had not yet returned. We met the other two girls in the program and then were interviewed by the front-line worker who who would be overseeing Kirstin's settling in. Then came the hardest part – time for me to leave. Kirstin cried and I cried. She begged to come home with me. *She would change. She would go to school. Things would be like they used to be before this terrible thing had happened to us.* But I had to refuse. I had to leave her there.

I cried uncontrollably as I drove home. Due to summer camp beginning as soon as her probationary period was over, she would not be coming home for several months, although we would be able to visit her on Sunday evenings, once she was settled into the program, and to see her during family therapy appointments.

The first few weeks were the toughest. It seemed as if she would never accept being there, but gradually she began to trust the child-care workers and the school teachers and even the other teens in the program. The first breakthrough came when the front-line worker, during the second weekend, managed to get Kirstin involved in a conversation about England. Her parents were English and came from the Surrey town where I had lived as a teenager and, like Kirstin, she had regularly visited her grandparents there. Kirstin relaxed as they exchanged experiences and, later in the day, progressed to participating the weekend activities.

"Dianne says the hurricane knocked down all the beech trees in Waller Lane. Isn't that terrible?" Kirstin said as soon as I arrived on my first Sunday evening visit.

Without knowing it, Dianne had stumbled on the right appeal. Kirstin cared more for trees than she did for people. The lines at the beginning of this chapter are from her narrative poem, *The Trees*, which tells the story of trees witnessing man's destruction of the earth. Feeling sorry about the trees took precedence over feeling sorry for herself. We were over the first hurdle. Slowly, Kirstin began to respond to the program and the people around her.

At last, towards the end of May, she was given an afternoon pass and she and Robbie and I (and Buffy) visited the current exhibition at the McMichael Collection of Canadian Art in Kleinburg and took Buffy for a walk along the trail by the Humber River, then played tennis at a nearby court. We were late getting her back because of a traffic accident which caused a major backup on the highway when we drove back to the city. When we finally did get back, Kirstin quite happily chatted to her child-care worker about the exhibition and the smashed up cars we'd seen on the highway.

The next Friday I picked her up and she and Robbie went to see a movie while I shopped for some items she needed for camping that weekend. After supper at a Yorkville bistro, she began to object to returning to the Hincks. She wanted to come home with us. I unhappily embarked on the now perfected, but painful, lecture about how much I wanted her to come home, but knew that residential treatment was the only way she was going to be able to conquer the awful fear that was destroying her life. As usual it was inadequate to the task of convincing her and she ran off when we got out of the car. It was an hour later before Robbie and I and one of the social workers managed to persuade her return to the building.

By the beginning of June, Kirstin had become used to her surroundings and fellow students. When they embarked on a Junior Achievement program, she was eager to exhibit her knowledge of the marketing process in selling the spray-painted t-shirts they produced and sold to their families, friends and staff members. She played her guitar and wrote and took part in revue sketches on talent nights. Her teacher admired her poetry to the extent of submitting some of it for inclusion in an anthology. Then, for the first time, she experienced the death of somebody she knew well.

Marion had been a second mother to both Kirstin and Robbie, taking care of them while I was working, for several years when they were younger. She had been the person to whom we turned when I had been hospitalized and had nobody to look after the children. Robbie and her youngest daughter, Barbara, had been friends almost all their lives and Kirstin and Barbara's older sister, Pamela, had been best friends from kindergarten days until the advent of Kirstin's social phobia. Ever since Marion had been diagnosed with a brain tumour the previous autumn, I had tried, in a low key manner, to prepare my children for the inevitable.

Having to break the news to Kirstin at a family therapy session was not easy. Confronting death for the first time and losing somebody who is an integral part of our childhood years is hard for all of us – and, for Kirstin, those years when she spent so much time at Marion's house, playing with her best friend, Pamela, belonged to the time before fear devastated her childhood. And, to make matters worse, Marion's death coincided with Kirstin's first experience of painful teenage love.

Since participants in the program were there to work out their social behaviour difficulties, involvement, even a same sex friendship, was not encouraged for the simple reason that there were problems enough in learning to control one's own condition without taking on those of somebody else. There had been several letter passing incidents and on the evening before Marion's funeral, the boy ran away after both he and Kirstin were put out of group for breaking the rules once again. This development was not made known to me until I arrived to pick Kirstin up to go to the funeral and, naturally, it resulted in the morning becoming even more charged with emotion than was expected. Rod Stewart (Marion was from

KIRSTIN'S STORY: *no place to stand*

Glasgow) recordings were played as background music and Kirstin and Pamela cried in each others' arms for their lost childhood.

After the funeral service, we set off to drive Kirstin back to the city. She announced that she was not going back. It was bad enough being there and not allowed to go home but, without Jason, life there would be totally unbearable. We were all, of course, feeling pretty grief-stricken after the funeral – it was not fair that a life should end at the age of forty-two, that four teenage girls should be left without a mother – and I tried to make Kirstin understand that decisions should never be made when emotions are running high. She threatened to jump out of the car. Robbie took care of keeping the doors locked and I kept driving as we argued. I kept driving, not wanting to risk another running away incident, eventually stopping at a restaurant for cold drinks, after judging the worst of Kirstin's hysteria to be over . Emotionally spent and continuing to make token protests, she eventually agreed to go back.

The Jason affair did not end there, however. He was reinstated in the program in time for summer camp which began the next week. Many of the camp activities kept the girls and boys separated, but the note passing continued and, at one point, I received a telephone call to let me know that Kirstin and Jason had run away from camp. They were found and brought back quite quickly.

It seemed an eternity to me, waiting by the phone – a different kind of anxiety, however, for this was a normal teenage escapade in comparison to the usual worries I had about my phobic child. Kirstin's asthma must have scared Jason, since the next time he ran away, he went alone and stayed away.

By family visiting day in late July, Kirstin and the other three girls in the program were happily hating camp life just like any other teenagers at any other summer camp. She showed us the nearby hiking trails and we drove over to Wasaga Beach for the afternoon – Buffy, too, because Family Day included family dogs!

The program returned to its city quarters in late August. The first weekend we were able to take Kirstin to a Blue Jays game and visit the Canadian National Exhibition, but she was not yet able to come home. The next weekend she came home on a day pass and went back in the evening. It was wonderful having her home again. I had redecorated her bedroom during the summer and, naturally, she spent quite some time rearranging the furniture to her own satisfaction. She and Robbie had lots of catching up to do, having (apart from the evening at the theatre in early June) only seen each other in the company of their parents for so many months. She was not exactly enthusiastic about going back, but she co-operated when it was time to drive her back to the city.

On the first couple of occasions that she had weekend

overnight passes, we managed to get her back to the Hincks... On the third Sunday evening, she ran away to avoid going back. She 'phoned me later that night – after I had resorted to seeking police help – and, relieved, I went and picked her up, but no amount of persuasion would get her back into treatment. She celebrated her sixteenth birthday that November which meant that there was no longer any legal necessity to attend school, eliminating the only effective means I had of making her participate in residential or any other kind of treatment program.

I made an abortive attempt to enrol her in the local high school. She actually felt quite comfortable about going there and we had an interview with the vice-principal and even set up a timetable with the guidance counsellor assigned to her. The following morning fear returned. All the new-found confidence was gone. She was unable to find the courage to get out of bed, much less go to school.

In January, she began to work on her high school credits by correspondence and spent more and more time alone – writing poetry and playing her guitar.

* * * * *

8

*I was diagnosed as having an anxiety-
related phobia leading to agoraphobia.
This was around Christmas '87. I
accepted the label thankfully. I used to go
into landslide depression frequently. It
was maddening that the doctors had
spent so many years labelling me as
depressive without trying to find out
what caused it. It was, of course, the
anxiety.*

from a letter of April, 1989

On several occasions in the past, I had considered
applying to the Ministry of Education for Kirstin to be
enrolled in correspondence education – particularly on
the occasions when even expensive private schools failed
to provide an environment which was not threatening to
her. I always concluded, however, that such a step would
only reinforce the isolation caused by her disorder. So,
instead, I would continue the search for a school where
she would not feel threatened. I never found one.

Unfortunately, by November 1988, when Kirstin
became sixteen, this dilemma had resulted in a sporadic
high school career spanning two schools, two long periods
in hospital school-rooms and the school program at the

Hincks Centre. Consequently Kirstin had never had the opportunity to complete a credit course – in essence, she had been continually starting the same grade nine courses over and over again. Upon enrolment, at this time, in Ministry of Education correspondence courses, she was, yet again, forced to take courses that she had started several times before. The resulting boredom hindered concentration and working on academic courses progressed slowly. Elective courses proved more interesting, but Kirstin's perfectionism – often a trait of social phobic people – prevented her from sending in her assignments unless she was convinced no further improvements could be made. Then, there was the frightening problem of having to sit with an invigilator for two hours, writing an exam.

Progress was slow and, eventually, her own reading – which was extensive, her writing and her art and music took precedence. In the face of the obvious, I failed miserably in my attempts to present high school credit courses as interesting and challenging and Kirstin preferred to invest her time in educating herself. Concerned about stress leading to depression again, I didn't press her but, at the same time, I was afraid that depression would, eventually, result from the unavoidable isolation.

Spring Break extended into the Easter weekend that year providing an opportunity to visit England, while fares were still off-peak, without having to take Robbie out of school. Due to school fees and other expenses, including the visit to my parents in Australia five years before, we had not been able to go to England since the summer of 1980. Kirstin had many memories of that trip, but Robbie had been only four at the time and remembered little of it. Kirstin, in recent years, had become very enthusiastic about claiming her British roots. She was an ardent fan of British television comedies and mystery fiction. Robbie was more interested in the British music scene. The children were not, however, the primary reason for our visit to England in 1989.

My parents were not very happy in their retirement in Australia and my mother, particularly, longed to get back to England. Mrs. Thatcher's England was no longer the place they knew and investigating the cost, in terms of housing, from the other side of the world was difficult for them. They were not of a generation which took risks and, since we were overdue for a holiday, it seemed to be a good idea to visit our relatives and look at the changed economy of Britain, at the same time.

I made reservations for the first few nights at a London hotel so that we could go sightseeing and to the theatre. Our early morning arrival meant that there were several hours before we were able to register at our hotel so, leaving our luggage at King's Cross railway station, we walked along to Madame Tussaud's Wax Museum to begin our sojourn as tourists. It was a great success. I hadn't been there myself since the Chamber of Horrors was the highlight of a visit with my father when I was nine years old. My children were quite a lot older than I was then, and had had a much more sophisticated upbringing which meant that the Chamber of Horrors impressed them far less than the more recent additions of nineteen eighties' rock musicians!

We did many of the things we had done on previous visits to London when we had taken the train up for the day from my parents' home in Surrey. This time, the children were older and we didn't have to worry about catching trains or not being late for supper. Instead, we had restaurant meals and went to the theatre. Kirstin was entranced by the London production of *Les Misérables* despite our long distance view from the back of the gallery – the only available seats. She was transported to that magical plateau I used to reach myself in London theatres when I was sixteen. It made me feel rather jaded but it was wonderful to see how it affected her. Robbie, still suffering jetlag, fell asleep!

The really wonderful thing about our trip to England was Kirstin telling me that, despite not having seen the friends and relatives we visited, since long before we'd ever heard of anxiety disorders, she was completely comfortable throughout the entire trip. No fear at all! In retrospect, I have often wondered if I was, perhaps, face-to-face with a solution and failed to recognize it. Not only did she not experience even a palpitation, she actually discussed her problem, on two separate occasions, with relatives she had not seen for years and hardly really knew. A voluminous correspondence, which continued until her death, resulted from an afternoon spent with a second cousin whom she had not seen since a visit to England nearly twelve years before.

England was wonderful. We were happy driving around the Sussex countryside visiting the sights of my own childhood memories and those of the children on earlier visits, eating lunch at country pubs, walking on the downs, along the sea-front and on the cliffs... and tearing Robbie away from the penny arcades on Brighton's Palace Pier.

Happy holidays must come to an end and we were soon home again. Robbie, now in junior high school, had made new friends. Kirstin had always tended to adopt a big sister attitude towards her brother's friends and, although it was probably a little patronizing, it did prevent her from succumbing to the fear that stood between her and teens of her own age. One Saturday morning I had taken my car to be serviced and called home to let the children know I was going to be longer than I had anticipated. Kirstin was having a panic attack and, according to Robbie, was in a foetal position in the corner of my basement study. His friend had brought his older brother over, but nobody had said or done anything to her – honestly! My car was finally in the service bay – there was no way for me to go home now. I told him to leave her completely alone and either ask the boys to go home or keep them away from her. The boys were shaken by the experience themselves and had left by the time I returned. Kirstin, herself, had recovered and gone to her room. Robbie complained about the embarrassment – why should she start freaking out on his friends now? I asked him about the friend's brother. He was a seventeen-year-old called Bobby.

Bobby, once recovered from witnessing Kirstin's panic attack, developed an infatuation for her and sought out her company. His continual visits – with or without his brother – resulted in her becoming used to him and, in fact, he and his brothers spent most of the summer with Kirstin and Robbie. Although not as attracted to Bobby as he was to her, Kirstin's morale was greatly boosted by the attentions of this boy who drenched himself in cologne for her and brought her flowers and chocolates. War games were high profile that summer and Kirstin, an expert on fantasy games whether of the board game or computerized variety, proved to be no less adept at organizing these live adaptations. She spent several weeks devising a very successful war game which became the highlight of the summer.

As the summer drew to a close, it became apparent

that my father, who had not been in very good health for several months, was seriously ill. My mother telephoned me to say he was scheduled to go into hospital for tests. She had never settled properly in Australia, finding it difficult to make friends and, consequently, was having a great deal of difficulty coping with my father's illness. She needed her family. For several years, there had been little communication between my parents and my sister and her family, now living further up the New South Wales coast, and the whereabouts of my brother - who had a habit of dropping out of sight every now and again - was not currently known to any of us. Kirstin, Robbie and I were all she had left for the time being. We would have to somehow get ourselves to Australia for Christmas.

* * * * *

9

*I'm progressing from fearing the world to
hating it... well, not the world itself, but
the power it has and the way it hurts me. I
sort of pity it, but my being terrified of
becoming part of it, pushes the pity aside.*

from of a letter of January, 1990.

Even before I had booked our tickets, the diagnosis
was made – lymphatic cancer. It would be my father's last
Christmas. Due to the distances involved in visiting
them, my children had never known my parents well.
When they lived in England we were able to visit them
every two or three years but, after they retired to Australia
late in 1981, we had managed to make the trip to see them
only once. The children and I were all in agreement – we'd
find the money to get there and make Grandad's last
Christmas a real one, with grandchildren in attendance
and a Christmas morning present-opening ceremony.

By December, he was home again, in the apartment
which we had visited six years before, and being taken by
ambulance to hospital for chemotherapy once a week. I
hoped he'd find our being there a diversion from the
monotony and pain of living with cancer. We arrived in

Sydney on Christmas Eve and, despite losing my way a few times (the Sydney roads were very confusing, then, for someone used to a North American city), I managed to drive the rented car through the city and suburbs, and on to Campbelltown. The town had changed quite a lot since our previous visit but, between the three of us, we figured out the way to my parents' unit, as apartments are called in Australia.

My mother must have been watching for us all morning. She was on her balcony as soon as we pulled into the parking lot behind the building, motioning us to the correct parking space. We carried our bags up, passing the swimming pool which did not look very well maintained now and the electric meter cupboard which seemed to have shrunk tremendously since the day Robbie had hidden in it, becoming the object of his grandmother's anger for the first and only time in his life – he was her favourite grandchild, and the anger had been brought about by fear of his being electrocuted. Mum's lifelong mistrust of electricity extended even to meters.

My father was sleeping, but lunch had been saved for us. I apologised for getting lost and taking so long. The children were not really terribly hungry but, remembering that Nana tended to get offended if you did not eat what she had made for you, sat down to lunch while my mother showed me which drawers and closet space we should use... and cried at the relief of having someone to share the pain for a while, at least.

My father was very frail and old. He was happy to see us, though a little overwhelmed by the teenaged grandchildren he had not seen for so long. Formerly an enthusiastic participant in community theatre, he brought out all his scrapbooks for Kirstin to read through and enjoyed reliving his triumphs as he expanded on the content of the newspaper clippings and programmes.

The next day, I found it hard not to remember other happier Christmas mornings as we took turns to open the presents. There were the sometimes poverty-stricken ones of my childhood which, nevertheless, were happy; the more adult and affluent ones when my sister and I were older and could contribute; the ones of my own children's early years, which would have shocked my parents – when first Kirstin and, later, Robbie were deluged with presents from my in-laws; the more recent ones in front of the fireplace in our pretty Streetsville home. We worked hard at making this one happy, too. Just as I had done, my mother had bought several small gifts for each of us in order to make the ceremony last as long as possible.

I had specifically rented a car with air conditioning in the hope that my father would be able to come out with us, but he preferred to stay at home, mostly watching television or sleeping. I was, at least, able to take my mother shopping, however, saving her the walk to the supermarket and waiting for groceries to be delivered.

Mostly, the children and I visited tourist attractions and beaches during the daytime and spent the evenings with my parents.

Kirstin enjoyed being in Australia again and, as with our visit to England earlier in the year, was free from fear throughout the trip. It was not until I was back in Australia, when my father died the following Easter, that I found out just how deeply her grandfather's dying affected her. Meantime, however, she spent most of her money on a leather hat which she bought during a trip in the Blue Mountains, swam and body-surfed happily in the warm South Pacific water and enthusiastically visited bird and animal sanctuaries. Robbie tended to be a little sulky at times – at thirteen, he was beginning to be self-conscious about being seen with his mother and sister even if there was nobody he knew to see him! But Kirstin absorbed Australia, just as she had soaked up the atmosphere in England, at Easter, and was happy there.

The three weeks passed too quickly. On our last evening there, my mother took her grandchildren to see a movie and I watched television with my father. Years before, when I was in my early teens and we, at last, had a television set, he had instilled in me a love of the films of his own youth in the nineteen thirties. So, the last time I watched a movie with my father, we saw the 1939 Paul Muni film, *'We Are Not Alone'*. My father, dying of cancer in Australia, in early 1990, was still very much the mannered colonial (he grew up in South Africa) gentleman of the nineteen-thirties.

"You see," he said, "there's no need for the explicit bilge that passes for acting today – a curtain blowing in the wind conveys the action..."

I found it a little ironic that he should find acceptable a story line about a man cheating on his wife – to the extent of getting himself charged with her murder – but drew the line at any possibility of watching him do it! I wondered, yet again, what had attracted him to Australia – hardly a country of people renowned for good taste and gentle living. I laughed and said I hoped the Mum wouldn't be too shocked by the movie she had taken the children to see. He said he thought it was 'some historical thing'.

"No, Dad," I said. "It's just called 'The Wars of the Roses'. It's about a marriage breaking up. Don't worry – it's supposed to be quite funny, but I don't think it's quite Mum's thing."

"That's pretty funny," he said, smiling, "she thought she was doing something educational with Kirstin and Robbie. But, perhaps, these days that sort of thing *is* education..."

We both laughed.

The next afternoon it was time to leave. My children never saw either of their grandparents again and I only saw them in the very last stages of their lives.

I drove to the airport in a blinding rainstorm which then proceeded to follow us to Auckland, Los Angeles and, even, Toronto, where the snow was all washed away and replaced by cold, heavy rain. The children didn't mind the rain – they were able to devote themselves to the acoustic guitars, the Christmas gifts that had been too big to take with us.

The week before the following Easter, in response to my mother's telephone call, I made the journey once again. My sister, Lorna had arrived a day ahead of me from Coffs Harbour on the northwest coast. She told me that my mother had shown her a beautiful letter Kirstin had written to Dad and – too shy to actually give it to him – had left in his room when we left for the airport three months before. My mother had, apparently, found it first and – still being at the stage of denying that her husband of forty-six years was terminally ill – had kept it from him. I was reluctant to broach the subject with my mother, but Lorna insisted she show me the letter. It was beautiful – classically beautiful in it's deep compassion, reassurance and understanding of impending death. Such a letter from a seventeen-year-old to her dying grandfather was beyond my mother's comprehension. My poor Kirstin. My poor father. That communication meant so much and now it was too late... he had spoken his last words soon after I arrived.

"You mustn't cry, Jean," he had said in a low voice that

seemed to come from deep within his emaciated body making it even more difficult than it would otherwise have been to do as he said.

During those few days before his death, both Lorna and I told him about the letter as we sat beside him in turn, hoping, perhaps, that it would help him to accept the death that he was, even then, fighting so hard. He died late in the evening of Maundy Thursday. I never told Kirstin what had happened with the letter – just that I had read it and that both Lorna and I thought it was the most beautiful gift she could have given him. And it truly was.

Robbie stayed with his father while I was in Australia, but Kirstin remained home and looked after the house. She had been really well for several months now. Admittedly, we were avoiding all the kinds of situations which would have created anxiety or caused panic attacks. She seemed to be feeling good about herself and concerned about me. When I returned from Australia, I found myself leaning on her in my grief over my father's illness and death and some unfortunate misunderstandings due to my mother's reaction to grief. That was not something I should have allowed to happen. I think it was the stress caused by what was, in fact, a sustained effort not to add to my burdens that caused her to suddenly plunge into deep depression a few weeks later.

Her grandfather's death impacted upon Kirstin far more than it really should have done because of the abrupt change in my parents' attitude towards life after their retirement and emigration to Australia. The grandfather who she had visited as a little girl, every two or three years in England, had played with her and read to her and made her feel good about herself. But the grandfather she visited in Australia was an old man already waiting for death in 1983 and facing the end of life in 1989. For Kirstin, this presented too many questions about the meaning of life. At the end of May she attempted suicide by overdosing on an asthma medication again.

I took her to our local hospital. This was a new facility to which I had twice taken Kirstin when we had not been able to get asthma attacks under control. I had not been very impressed by its psychiatric department on the occasions when I had come into contact with it. One of these was prior to Kirstin's hospitalization at Sunnybrook when I had not even managed to make contact with the doctor to whom our family physician had referred her. My immediate concern was in obtaining medical assistance but, once her condition was stabilized, a hospital psychiatrist was, of course, called in to see her. I arrived to visit her during the first consultation and was surprised and pleased to see her laughing quite happily with him, appearing to be quite comfortable as she gave him her history.

Kirstin agreed to begin psychotherapy with the psychiatrist and our family doctor, who – after more than eight years – finally agreed that Kirstin had a problem and arranged for access to the public health department which provided regular visits to our home by both a public health nurse and an occupational therapist and immediate eligibility to a transitional group therapy program for Kirstin.

It was truly amazing to suddenly find all these resources available in our own community after so many years of being told they did not exist. Maybe that sounds a little cynical. Perhaps it was only because she would soon be eighteen and eligible for adult services.

Kirstin, then, was within a few months of her eighteenth birthday when we finally obtained an effective combination of psychotherapy, group and occupational therapy, plus the additional comfort – from my own point of view – of the public health nurse dropping by from time to time. To begin with I drove her to and from the hospital for both the appointments with the psychiatrist and for the group therapy sessions. Then, gradually, with the help of the occupational therapist, she was able to make the short bus trip to attend the Monday morning and Thursday afternoon groups and the six-week anxiety management course she took on Wednesday evenings in the Fall. Soon, she made friends with and, in fact, became something of a surrogate daughter to a participant of the Thursday afternoon group, who would pick her up and bring her home by car.

Compassionate by nature, Kirstin became concerned with the various problems of the people attending the three programs in which she was taking part. They were adults with various psychological and/or physical conditions which caused psychological problems. Other than the young adults she had met during the two months she had spent in the evaluation program at Sunnybrook, she had always been in treatment with young people of her own age – and it was fear of her peers that created the most panic for Kirstin. Reaching a comfort level with the adults in these groups came relatively quickly and she was able to relax and participate within a few weeks. The regular contact with older people attempting to control or overcome their problems had far more impact upon her than any previous treatment program. She became quite involved in their various situations and was exposed for the first time to intellectual discussion on the advantages and disadvantages of the pharmacological and psychotherapeutic approaches to treating the variety of nervous and psychological disorders from which they were suffering. In familiar surroundings with people who she did not find threatening, Kirstin was a very articulate person who could comprehensively discuss any subject with which she was conversant. Over the years she had spent – since she was alone so much – far more time reading and studying than most children do, so that by this time, she had accumulated quite a storehouse of knowledge on some of the disorders affecting her fellow group members, and their various psychological effects. She became accepted her as something of an authority on such topics. Being perceived in this manner, instead of being considered to be a naive teenager, increased her self-esteem immeasurably.

The psychiatrist, however – as is the habit of health professionals – did not share the same respect for the depth of her research, and accepting responsibility for attending group therapy did not extend to Kirstin keeping her appointments with him. Soon, there were problems. At first, with one or two exceptions, I was able to persuade her to attend and, upon the psychiatrist's recommendation in September, she agreed to resume taking the tricyclic antidepressant/anti-anxiety medication, imipramine. This, combined with the self-esteem which was developing as a result of her involvement in group therapy and the anxiety management course, assisted Kirstin in taking control of her life again. It also led to her becoming increasingly disillusioned with the psychiatrist.

* * * * *

10

Come Alive

Darkness falls,
descending sky
the clouds are falling.
Come alive.

Teardrops on the border line
Drifting over seas of mind
On your right what's left behind
On your left the other side.
Come alive.

Much of the improved outlook on life Kirstin was experiencing, by the Autumn of 1990, was expressed in an increased devotion to music. She and Robbie began working together on their guitars – to the extent of even taking lessons together. They bought a mixer, set up speakers and moved Robbie's drums into Kirstin's basement studio, henceforth to be known as the Music Room. They were both intensely interested in New Age doctrines, the Bhagavad Gita, *I Ching* and vegetarianism. Kirstin went with her father to see the Dalai Lama, during his 1990 visit to Toronto, and became increasingly involved in studying eastern religions and metaphysics. She wrote a lot, too – mostly poetry, sometimes with music and she still sketched and painted. I gave up trying to get her to work on her high school credits – maybe she was intellectually on a higher plane or, perhaps, now that Robbie was in high school it was a form of withdrawal from what, in essence, would have been competition (something both she and Robbie had always tended to avoid both in terms of competing with each other and competing with others). Whatever it was, except for a few half-hearted attempts made mainly to please me, she was not interested in working on high school credits.

In Australia, my nephew, Kevin, who intended to become a graphic designer, began working on a community magazine and asked Kirstin to write a monthly column from the viewpoint of a Canadian teenager. Kirstin set to work enthusiastically creating a little beaver mascot, wearing skates and sporting a hockey stick, named Buck Cannuck to head up the column, and became *The Canadian Connection* writing about Canadian youth and music for readers in Coffs Harbour, New South Wales.

Despite becoming disenchanted with the psychiatrist – who, she said, lacked knowledge and understanding of anxiety disorders – and her subsequent reluctance to keep appointments, Kirstin's self image continued to improve. By Christmas, her confidence level was high enough to justify an investment in driving lessons as her major gift. The Young Drivers of Canada program provides a payment program that would allow me to cut my losses if she was unable to handle the twice weekly classroom lessons. However, she controlled her fear and attended the four weeks of lessons, actually made a friend among her classmates, obtained her 365-day licence and moved on to her in-car sessions.

During a visit to some friends with her father in January, Kirstin renewed acquaintance with a boy of her own age who she had played with as a small child. Encouraged by their fathers, it soon developed into another case of the same intense teenage passion she had experienced for the boy who had participated in the Hincks program two years before. For several weeks she was blissfully happy, but he – another Jason – lived sixty miles away and, at eighteen, did not yet have the capacity to maintain an enduring long distance relationship. Amazingly, after the initial heartbreak of the weekend when she discovered that there were other girls in Jason's life, Kirstin seemed to recover quite quickly and the emotional trauma did not impact greatly on her hard won self-confidence. She continued in successfully controlling her disorder.

In February my mother, now living in England again, was hospitalized after several episodes of fainting and dizziness. By the end of the month, inoperable abdominal cancer had been diagnosed. After a telephone discussion with her doctor, I arranged to fly to England immediately.

Because of Kirstin's suicide attempt in the aftermath of my father's death, I was terrified of the impact of my mother's illness and death on me producing stress for my daughter – especially now, after the months spent in strengthening her fragile ego. As it turned out, there was not the same level of shock this time for either Kirstin or myself. My mother had never reconciled herself to my father's death so, while we felt sad over her impending death, for her, perhaps, it was best. I just wished that it was due to a cause other than cancer – both from the point of view of the pain and because my poor mother, even after having her incontestably absolutely-always-scrubbed-and-clean husband die from it, still had the old-fashioned idea that cancer was caused by lack of hygiene.

That weekend, I stocked up on food that the children could prepare easily, alerted their father and wrote out instructions for surviving any catastrophe that could possibly happen but, otherwise, made a concerted effort to behave as if nothing out of the ordinary was happening. I took Kirstin out for driving practice on the cold Sunday afternoon before my evening flight.

The prognosis was that my mother had, possibly, three months to live, so I decided that I would just have to commute back and forth in order to spend time with her, be home with Kirstin and Robbie and keep up with my work. After getting my mother discharged from the hospital, I settled her in the apartment in the seniors' development where she lived, supervised her medications until she could manage the schedule herself and ensured that a support system of neighbours and relatives was in place. I left intending to be back again a couple of weeks later, but I never saw her alive again. I booked my next trip for the Monday after Easter and phoned her every morning to make sure she was all right. I had been home a little more than a week when she told me, over the phone, that she was going into a hospice – but just to recover her strength. When I phoned the hospice each morning, I was told that the phone in her room was 'still out-of-order' and given contradicting reports on the state of her health, but was assured that she'd be fine by the time I got back there again and advised to keep my flight booking as it was. Finally, after my mother had been there for a week, I was told she was fading fast, by which time – just days before the Easter weekend – it was impossible to change my flight or get another one. I called my brother with the update and, thankfully, he arrived at the hospice before she died on Maundy Thursday– just as my father had done the previous year.

All this created stress for me, but Kirstin wrote in her diary; *"Nana died. It was really just as well that she did not suffer long, as Grandad did. She has passed over into another world where she will no longer have to struggle..."*

During the weeks before and after my mother's death, Kirstin really seemed to be taking control of her life. After some initial shyness, she became comfortable with her driving instructor and took pride in driving my car or her father's whenever the opportunity arose. She worked temporarily for the electronic component distributor where her father was employed at the time. She assisted in assembling equipment and was given clerical tasks and, keeping her anxiety well under control, experienced the conflicts and gossip of the workplace for the first time. The girls she was working with were several years older than she was so there was none of the old fear of peers to be confronted. They liked her and found her interesting. She had become quite an expert on *I Ching*, by this time, and could read tarot cards, which attracted the attention of the other girls – especially after Kirstin told them things about themselves which she could not possibly have known!

Apart from my mother's illness and death and my trips to England, life was almost normal during the Spring of 1991. Two or three days a week, Kirstin would drive to the subway to drop Robbie off to go to his school in the city, then to the office where she was working. I would, then, take over and drive to my own office and we'd reverse the process for the journey home. She felt good about herself and would, perhaps, have continued to do so but, unfortunately, office politics resulted in her father leaving the company on bad terms with the owner and Kirstin feeling too uncomfortable to stay.

Then, all at once, the entire support system began to crumble. The transition therapy groups were cancelled after one of the facilitators left for another job and the other went on maternity leave. Worst of all a misunderstanding, which I did not find out about until several months later, resulted in the termination of the occupational therapist's visits. I discovered, while seeing our family doctor for my own annual physical, that somehow a clerical error had turned Kirstin's therapeutic temporary, part-time job into a full-time career and eliminated her eligibility for occupational therapy. At the beginning of May, it was not a major problem... by October, it was a matter of life or death.

Kirstin bought a new guitar with some of the money she earned from her temporary job. Perhaps if she had bought the guitar somewhere else, things would not have changed... Then again, perhaps if the group therapy program had not been cancelled, or if the occupational therapist's visits had not been terminated or if fear of the examiner, during her driving test, had not resulted in her failing to see the red light... I suppose the real problem was that all these things happened at the same time.

We had made several previous purchases at the musician's supply store where Kirstin bought her new guitar – particularly during the early days when first

Kirstin, then Robbie, took guitar lessons and broken strings were a continual hazard. Kirstin mostly played an electric guitar but Robbie, who had only in recent months become a serious guitar player, preferred an acoustic instrument. He had, himself, upgraded from his original inexpensive acoustic guitar and, now, talked Kirstin into buying a steel string instrument. The purchase of the guitar included some free lessons and Kirstin, surprisingly – since she was comfortable with the teacher with whom she had studied for several years and really didn't need them – returned to the store's studio for the lessons. The owner, a keen mentor of many of his young customers, encouraged her to continue to visit.

He meant to be kind, of course, but had no idea of the effort it cost Kirstin to even enter the store – let alone 'casually' hang around the studio. I would hear her shallow breathing as we drove to the music store on Saturday afternoons and, although I appreciated the value of desensitization therapy, I was afraid she was pushing herself too hard. But she was infatuated by one of the young men who was employed to give lessons at the studio and was determined to be accepted as a fellow musician. I think she spent most of the time she was there desperately fighting to control her panic, which meant that conversation became physically difficult, while being left to her own devices, when everybody was busy, was just as threatening. Each time I picked her up she was as white as a sheet and one day I had to stop the car because she was throwing up. After that, I called the owner of the store and explained about Kirstin's disorder. He was concerned and aspired to be helpful, but – like most people – had no idea of the impact of inconsistency upon anxiety disorders. She was excited and felt complimented when he suggested she take singing lessons from him, then he failed to be there the next weekend. Such instability and, for Kirstin, the added fear of rejection made it even more difficult for her to find the courage to go there again.

School ended for Robbie, in the middle of June. He and Kirstin, together with a friend of his from school went on a week's hiking trip. They returned home tanned and healthy but, cleaning and putting their equipment away, I went through the medications Kirstin had taken with her and discovered that she had not been taking her anti-depressants.

"I decided not to take them any more," she said. "I want to be happy the natural way."

I'm the last person to dispute such a wish but Kirstin knew, as well as I did, that imipramine is drug that the system must be weaned from. The very fact that she had simply stopped taking it, with no regard to this, suggested depressive thinking. Even using the weaning procedure, under a psychiatrist's supervision, the last time she had stopped taking imipramine, a suicide attempt had been made. I tried to rationalize the situation with her but, already clinically depressed, she refused to discuss it. The psychiatrist said there was nothing he could do to help unless I got her to keep her appointments. Self-evident, yes – but hardly helpful.

Two weeks later, my father-in-law died in Nanaimo. He was my children's third grandparent to die in a fifteen month period. We attended his memorial service in Toronto. Listening to the tributes, I realised – too late – just how much impact this was going to have on Kirstin. It would have been better to have found some excuse for not attending despite the risk of creating inevitable misunderstandings with my in-laws.

The summer progressed and Kirstin fell deeper into depression and reclusivity, refusing both medication and co-operation in my attempts to have her admitted to hospital. After a night in late August spent wandering the countryside after writing a suicide note, she agreed to take her medication again but refused hospitalization. The hospital's crisis intervention team did not see her actions as meeting the requirements for a committal order on the grounds that she was a danger to herself. A second attempt to have her hospitalized failed a few weeks later, despite the catatonic state which had caused my son and I to force her into the car and down to the hospital again. I finally managed to have Kirstin admitted – as an involuntary patient on a committal order – at the end of October when she was, once again, catatonic as I literally dragged her to an appointment with her psychiatrist. However, again a perceived lack of indication that she was a danger to herself prevented the psychiatrist from extending the initial two week committal order. She was discharged by our family doctor, her fear of participation in group therapy seen as a refusal to co-operate with treatment and my own desperate efforts, to persuade her to stay, declined due to that same fear.

She died a week later while staying at her father's apartment. After a difference of opinion with him, she swallowed the remains of her two-week imipramine prescription while he slept in front of the television set.

She knew she should have stayed in the hospital. She had known it all the week. So had her father and they had both known that neither could cope with the other's fragile ego. The situation had derived from the combination of her own stubborn resolve to prove the hospital's incapacity to help her last week and his equally obstinate desire to give her what she wanted – whether or not it was what she needed. And she, also, knew that neither of them was going to admit to being wrong. So she would solve all the problems in this one step – he would be shown that she was prepared to die in order to provide a stimulus from which he could draw the strength to overcome his weakness, her mother would be happy that she was safely back in hospital, the doctors would be made to look like the fools they were for discharging her in the first place. And, if they did not get her to the hospital in time... well, that was all right, too.

She'd get to ultimate safety then, and need never be afraid again...

They did not get Kirstin to the hospital in time.

She was pronounced dead in the early hours of November 16th 1991, eight days after her nineteenth birthday. I never knew whether she actually died before or after midnight that night which is why only the years of her life are inscribed on her headstone – not the months and days. She spoke often of a place of eternal love and understanding, a place that she hoped to find where she need no longer struggle with the all-engulfing fear. She chose to find that place.

Kirstin's story of fighting fear took place over a period of ten years – ten years of fear, anxiety, panic depression and frustration for her and false hope and heartache for the rest of us. She cared passionately about people, about animals and about the environment but, for the most part, her condition allowed her to demonstrate her concern to the rest of the world only through the poetry and music she wrote. She saw herself as a twentieth century Elizabeth Barrett Browning but, unlike that earlier reclusive poet, she found no kindred spirit to assist her in escaping her bonds and finding her place to stand.

* * * * *

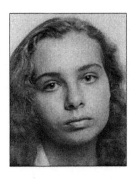

For ever and always may you sing of love.

* * * * *

After her daughter's death, Jean Jardine Miller published a book of Kirstin's poetry entitled, *Songs of My Soul*. Later, she launched *The Lifeline Anxiety Disorder Newsletter*, a quarterly print and internet publication providing news, views and commentary on anxiety disorders.

She lives in Halton Hills, Ontario.